EVIDENCE OF THE AFTERLIFE

EVIDENCE OF THE AFTERLIFE

The Science of Near-Death Experiences

Jeffrey Long, MD
with Paul Perry

HarperOne
An Imprint of HarperCollinsPublishers

HarperOne

HarperCollins books may be purchased for educational, business, or sales
promotional use. For information, please e-mail the Special Markets Department
at SPsales@harpercollins.com.

HarperCollins website: http://www.harpercollins.com

HarperCollins®, ■®, and HarperOne™ are trademarks of HarperCollins
Publishers.

FIRST HARPERCOLLINS PAPERBACK EDITION PUBLISHED IN 2011

Library of Congress Cataloging-in-Publication Data
    Long, Jeffrey, M.D.
        Evidence of the afterlife : the science of near-death experiences / by Jeffrey
Long, with Paul Perry. — 1st ed.
            p.   cm.
        ISBN 978–0–06–145257–4
        1. Near-death experiences. 2. Future life. I. Perry, Paul. II. Title.
    BF1045.N4L66 2010
    133.901'3—dc22   2009021251

24 25 26 27 28 LBC 34 33 32 31 30

DEDICATED TO THE THOUSANDS OF PEOPLE WHO HAVE SHARED THEIR EXCEPTIONAL EXPERIENCES WITH US OVER THE YEARS, AND TO THOSE WHO WILL SHARE IN THE FUTURE. YOU ARE AMONG THE GREATEST OF TEACHERS.

DEDICATED TO NEAR-DEATH-EXPERIENCE RESEARCHERS, PAST AND FUTURE.

DEDICATED TO JODY LONG, WHOSE EFFORTS MADE THIS BOOK POSSIBLE.

Contents

Contents

Introduction

A bit beyond perception's reach
I sometimes believe I see
that Life is two locked boxes, each
containing the other's key.
—Piet Hein

It was 1984 when I first stumbled upon the phrase *near-death experience* (NDE) in the pages of a medical journal. It was several years later that I heard a friend's wife tell of her own NDE when she nearly died of an allergic reaction while under general anesthetic. More than ten years later, in 1998, I started the Near Death Experience Research Foundation and its corresponding website, NDERF.org.

One of my goals for the site was to collect as many NDEs as I could and to collect them through a questionnaire that would make it easy to separate and study their elements. With such a questionnaire, I could examine the individual elements in NDEs or an entire NDE itself. I expected to be successful in an endeavor, but as it has turned out, I have been *wildly* successful. Over the course of the first ten years, more than 1,300 people who had a near-death experience spent many hours of their precious time answering over one hundred questions in NDERF's detailed questionnaire. These people are of every race, creed, and color and are from virtually every corner of the world.

That so many people are willing to share their NDEs with others speaks volumes about the power of these experiences in a person's life. Respondents describe their experiences in a variety of ways, calling them "unspeakable," "ineffable," "unforgettable," "beautiful beyond words," and so on. More than 95 percent of the respondents feel their NDE was "definitely real," while virtually all of the remaining respondents feel it was "probably real." Not one respondent has said it was "definitely not real." Some say it was not only the most real thing to ever happen to them but also the best event of their lives. As one respondent who nearly died in a suicide attempt wrote:

I was at peace with myself. Nothing hurt. I could only see my life and self through that Being's Love. There was no negative in myself or from that Being for anything I had done, including killing myself. It [my deed] was changed by the power of the Truth of Love, with which it was seen. That Loving Grace, total acceptance, complete love and truth created a joy in me. I saw that love was in me too, not just from the Being shining down on me; it was in me as part of myself. I was full of love and peace. I felt the joy in that truth. I have no right words for it.

I have seen this type of response from many people with near-death experiences. Imagine that—an experience that begins with the sheer terror of a life-threatening event and evolves into an event of wonder and mystery!

I am a man of science, and as a result I have examined the data from the NDERF study in a scientific way. At NDERF we explored *all* of the elements in the NDEs of more than one thousand people, examining consistency among the accounts. In reaching conclusions about these accounts, we followed a basic scientific principle: *What is real is consistently seen among many different observations.*

The results of the NDERF study clearly indicate remarkable consistency among NDE case studies. This study finds that what people discovered during their near-death experience about God, love, afterlife, reason for our earthly existence, earthly hardships, forgiveness, and many other concepts is strikingly consistent across cultures, races, and creeds. Also, these discoveries are generally not what would have been expected from preexisting societal beliefs, religious teachings, or any other source of earthly knowledge.

In a world that is plagued by afflictions of the soul, this is very good news. Many of the personal and social problems that face humanity—drug and alcohol abuse, depression, anxiety, gang violence, religious strife, racism, and so on—could be greatly affected by such a powerful common experience. Because NDEs happen to people all over the world, they are a spiritual thread that binds us together, a common experience that reminds us of our mutual spiritual nature. At its very least, the NDERF study contributes information that strengthens our understanding of that spiritual thread.

But the NDERF study is also exceptionally valuable in the way that it brings us closer to understanding what happens when we die. I long ago quit believing that death is the cessation of our existence. It took me a long time to reach this point. I was born into a scientific family. My father was the chair of the Department of Pharmacology at the University of Iowa and a onetime contender for the Nobel Prize. Through him and others in our family I developed great respect for science.

By scientifically studying the more than 1,300 cases shared with NDERF, I believe that the nine lines of evidence presented in this book all converge on one central point: *There is life after death.*

The convergence of several lines of evidence—like the nine presented in this book—builds a much stronger case than only a single line of evidence.

For example, suppose we had only two lines of NDE evidence. We may not be 100 percent convinced that these two lines of evidence prove an afterlife, but perhaps each line of evidence by itself is 90 percent convincing. Combined, these two lines of evidence by mathematical calculation are 99 percent convincing that the afterlife exists.[1]

Given how complex it is to mathematically analyze only *two* lines of evidence, imagine how mind-boggling it would be to mathematically analyze all *nine* lines of NDE evidence. Fortunately, that won't be necessary. The NDERF website includes a custom-designed form that automatically performs these mathematical calculations. This website wizardry allows *you* to calculate for yourself how strongly *you* believe the nine lines of evidence prove the existence of an afterlife. You can also see the results obtained from every other person who has completed this form. This form, and other material supplementing this book, is available on the NDERF website at our page that explores evidence of the afterlife (http://www.nderf.org/afterlife). The form addresses concepts presented throughout this book. Thus I would encourage you to finish reading this book before you complete the form.

WHAT HAPPENS DURING A NEAR-DEATH EXPERIENCE

Before continuing, I should provide a detailed explanation of what a near-death experience is.

Near-death experiences (NDEs) are events that take place as a person is dying or, indeed, is already clinically dead. People who have NDEs are called near-death experiencers (NDErs). From the time near-death experiences were first medically researched and described by Dr. Raymond Moody in his pioneering book, *Life After Life*, in 1975, medical doctors and other researchers have examined this phenomenon in depth.[2]

There is no widely accepted definition of near-death experience. The NDERF study took a straightforward approach by defining both the *near-death* and *experience* components of near-death experience. I considered individuals to be "near death" if they were so physically compromised that they would die if their condition did not improve. The NDErs studied were generally unconscious and often apparently clinically dead, with absence of heartbeat and breathing. The "experience" had to occur at the time they were near death. Also, the experience had to be lucid, to exclude descriptions of only fragmentary and disorganized memories.

Throughout this book we will present the results of the NDERF survey. Unless otherwise indicated, these will be the results from surveying 613 sequential NDErs who completed the most recent version of the NDERF survey.[3] This version of the survey included the NDE Scale questions.[4] The NDE Scale asks sixteen questions about the content of the experience and is the most validated research method to help distinguish experiences that are near-death experiences from those that are not. The 613 NDErs whose survey results we are presenting here all had NDE Scale scores of 7 or above, further validating these experiences as actual NDEs. The original version of the NDERF survey studied responses from 413 NDErs. The NDE Scale questions were not used in the original NDERF survey.

No two near-death experiences are identical. However, when many near-death experiences are studied, a pattern of elements that commonly occurs in NDEs is easily seen. These elements usually occur in consistent order.

Researchers have concluded that NDEs may include some or all of the following twelve[5] elements:[6]

1. Out-of-body experience (OBE): Separation of consciousness from the physical body
2. Heightened senses
3. Intense and generally positive emotions or feelings
4. Passing into or through a tunnel
5. Encountering a mystical or brilliant light
6. Encountering other beings, either mystical beings or deceased relatives or friends
7. A sense of alteration of time or space
8. Life review

9. Encountering unworldly ("heavenly") realms
10. Encountering or learning special knowledge
11. Encountering a boundary or barrier
12. A return to the body, either voluntary or involuntary

Below are descriptions of each of these elements from the case studies I have amassed over more than ten years of research, as well as the percentage of NDErs from our study group who experienced each of the elements.

1. Out-of-Body Experience (OBE)

I could feel my spirit actually leaving my body. I saw and heard the conversations between my husband and the doctors taking place outside my room, about forty feet away down a hallway. I was later able to verify this conversation to my shocked husband.

One NDEr observed in the out-of-body state the reaction of the doctor to nearly losing this patient:

Why were you so upset, screaming and swearing in the operating room? Didn't you know that I could hear every word you said?

This NDEr then shared what the doctor responded:

You are right. I was so frustrated and tired and angry in that operating room that I just started screaming when we were losing you. It was either scream or cry. You were dying, and there was not a damned thing that I could do to stop it. I will have to rethink what I say to an unconscious patient from now on, won't I?

Out-of-body experiences are often the first NDE element. The NDERF survey asked 613 NDErs, "Did you experience a separation of your consciousness from your body?" In response, 75.4 percent answered "Yes."

2. Heightened Senses

There isn't a way to explain it, as there is no feeling like it here on earth. It was crystal clear. It was like going home at last, at last. A feeling of belonging, of meaning, of completeness.

It just seemed so much more real than anything I had ever experienced in my entire life.

The NDERF survey asked, "How did your highest level of consciousness and alertness during the experience compare to your normal, everyday consciousness and alertness?" Of the NDErs surveyed, 74.4 percent indicated they had "More consciousness and alertness than normal."

3. Intense and Generally Positive Emotions or Feelings

This is the hardest thing to try and explain. . . . Words will not come close to capturing the feelings, but I'll try: total, unconditional, all-encompassing love, compassion, peace, warmth, safety, belonging, understanding, overwhelming sense of being home, and joy.

All I felt was love, joy, happiness, and every wonderful emotion you could feel all at once.

Total peace, total calm. I was not in the least bit afraid or anxious.

When we got to the light, the totality of life was love and happiness. There was nothing else. And it was intense. Very intense and endless in scope.

[I felt an e]xtreme sense of love and peace and beauty that I cannot describe in words.

The NDERF survey asked, "Did you have a feeling of peace or pleasantness?" To this question, 76.2 percent selected "Incredible peace or pleasantness." The NDERF survey asked another question about a specific emotion during the NDE: "Did you have a feeling of joy?" NDErs responded to this question with 52.5 percent selecting "Incredible joy."

A small percentage of NDEs are frightening to the NDEr. This topic is addressed in detail on the NDERF website.[7]

4. Passing Into or Through a Tunnel

My next awareness was of being submerged and cradled in a warm, wavy, wafting motion at the opening of a tunnel. The tunnel had billowy soft sides and was well lit, with the tunnel dimensions decreasing and brightness increasing as it got closer to a single bright light.

We traveled very fast into a tunnel. The tunnel was all different colors: blue, yellow, white, green, and red.

The NDERF survey asked, "Did you pass into or through a tunnel or enclosure?" Of NDErs responding to this survey question, 33.8 percent answered "Yes."

5. Encountering a Mystical or Brilliant Light

A brilliant white light at the end of the tunnel, and when the wings enveloped me I became part of the white light.

A beautiful light drew me to itself; the light still touches me with awe, and tears come immediately.

At first the light was blue. Then it transitioned to white. It was an opalescent white; it almost glowed, but did not shine. It was bright, but not intense bright, like glowing bright—pure bright. Pure but not in the usual sense of the word. Pure as in something you've never seen before or could ever describe or put into words.

It was as if we passed through a wall into my light pod directly. There was a large majestic center light and then the individual yet connected pod lights exactly like the center light only smaller. I think now the pod lights, like mine, were other souls connected to the center light, God.

The light may be described as brilliant, "like a million suns," but virtually never hurts the NDEr to look at it. NDErs may dramatically describe their strong attraction to the light and their emphatic desire to approach or merge with the light. The NDERF survey asked, "Did you see a light?" NDErs responded with 64.6 percent answering "Yes."

6. Encountering Other Beings, Either Mystical Beings or Deceased Relatives or Friends

I was surrounded by other beings, or people, who I felt as though I recognized. These beings were like family, old friends, who'd been with me for an eternity. I can best describe them as my spiritual or soul family. Meeting these beings was like reuniting with the most important people in one's life, after a long separation. There was an explosion of love and joy on seeing each other again between us all.

My dad was right next to me, but I couldn't see him visually. My sister was very close; I felt she was to my left. I felt other family members close by, but I did not see them. My sister and other family members seemed to be more to the left. The only person besides my sister and my dad that I knew was there was my grandmother. There were others there but none I can say for certain besides the ones I mentioned.

I heard my mother's and daughter's voices, but my daughter, who was only approximately two at the time, well, it was the sound of her voice grown up, but I knew it was her voice. They called my name, and my body moved like through an air current very quickly. It was like the wind carried me so fast, and I saw a bright, bright light very quickly and then a beach, and then I saw my mom and daughter standing on the beach; my daughter was grown up.

The NDERF survey asked, "Did you meet or see any other beings?" In response, 57.3 percent answered "Yes." When NDErs encounter deceased beings, most are deceased relatives as opposed to friends or loved ones. Some NDErs encounter seemingly familiar beings, but they cannot recall having previously met them. Later in their lives some NDErs recognize a picture of a deceased relative as the being they encountered in their NDE. The relative may have died years or even decades before the NDEr was born.

7. A Sense of Alteration of Time or Space

When I first left my body I had my diving watch on. I took some very unscientific measurements of the distance I traveled by watching for features and measuring them by the second hand on my watch. Totally unscientific. But my conclusion was and has always been: I was measuring time in an altered time. The ground never moved in a linear fashion; the distances were erratic at best. The distances were always changing, sometime[s] repeating and then instantly becom[ing] longer or short[er] than the previous distance. Yet my watch was always ticking without change. My intuition and impression were that I was in a different time zone, one where my earth[l]y watch was of no use or inept at making any measurement or reflecting time. Also without mistake I would say this whole thing took an hour or more. It seemed to me that I was in the NDE for a very long time. But when I asked my diving partners how long had I been unconscious, they estimated five to ten minutes. Thus I had another reason to support why my diving watch didn't seem to measure the time in my NDE.

It seemed as though I experienced so much in such a small length of earthly time. Where my soul had traveled to know nothing of time as we know [of] time passing on earth.

Both time and space in earth stopped completely. Simultaneously, "the time and the space" on the other side was completely alive, evident[ial], and real.

Yes, while I was in the light, I had . . . [no] sense of time as I know it here on Earth. In other words, no sense of the serial nature of time . . . past, present, or future. All times (past, present, and future) were experienced at every moment in time while I was in the light.

The NDERF survey asked, "Did you have any sense of altered space or time?" To this question the majority, 60.5 percent, answered "Yes." Another NDERF survey question focused only on an altered sense of time, asking, "Did time seem to speed up?" NDErs responded to this question with 33.9 percent selecting "Everything seemed to be happening all at once."

8. Life Review

I saw my life flash before me shortly after I left my body and was still in the hospital room. I was told that I was going to help educate and teach many people, and that is exactly what I am doing now.

I saw every important event that had ever happened in my life, from my first birthday to my first kiss to fights with my parents.

I saw how selfish I was and how I would give anything to go back and change.

Next he showed me my life review. Every second from birth until death you will see and feel, and [you will] experience your emotions and others that you hurt, and feel their pain and emotions. What this is for is so you can see what kind of person you were and how you treated others from another vantage point, and you will be harder on yourself than anyone to judge you.

I will not see what others have done to you. I will see what you have done to others.

Life reviews involve a review of prior events of the NDEr's life. Fragments of one's earthly life may be seen, or the review may be panoramic, covering all of one's earthly life. The NDERF survey asked, "Did you experience a review of past events in your life?" To that question, 22.2 percent of NDErs answered "Yes."

9. Encountering Unworldly ("Heavenly") Realms

Well, the end of that tunnel was the most peaceful place; it was beyond my imaginings, pure, serene, and loving.

The landscape was beautiful, blue skies, rolling hills, flowers. All was full of light, as if lit from within itself and emitting light, not reflecting it.

There was such beauty, beautiful beyond expression. There was also a bright city or something like a city in the distance. The colors and structures of everything [were] beautiful . . . awesome.

All around me I could see and feel a beautiful peace and tranquillity with love and peace. . . . As far as the eye could see to my left was a beautiful landscape of tulips of every color imaginable. To my right was a wall of a beautiful blue that matched the sky.

The sound of that music I cannot possibly describe with words because it simply cannot be heard with that clarity in this world! The colors were out of this world—so deep, so luminous, so beautiful!

The NDERF survey asked, "Did you see or visit any beautiful or otherwise distinctive locations, levels, or dimensions?" To this question 40.6 percent of NDErs chose "Yes." Asking this question in a more general way, the NDERF survey asked, "Did you seem to enter some other, unearthly world?" To this question 52.2 percent of NDErs responded that they encountered an unearthly realm.

10. Encountering or Learning Special Knowledge

When I looked into his eyes all the secrets of the universe were revealed to me. I know how everything works because I looked into his eyes for a moment. All the secrets of the universe, all knowledge of all time, everything.

I understood (I use this term because I did not actually hear) the colored drops were the experiences of all who had lived. The experiences existed as separate items yet belonged to the whole. The whole was the collective knowledge of all.

The NDERF survey asked, "Did you have a sense of knowing special knowledge, universal order, and/or purpose?"

To this question 56.0 percent of NDErs answered "Yes." Another question asked, "Did you suddenly seem to understand everything?" To this question, 31.5 percent responded that they seemed to understand everything "About the universe," and 31.3 percent responded that they seemed to understand everything "About myself or others."

11. Encountering a Boundary or Barrier

On my side of the boundary, time seemed to go slow. On the other side, time went by faster.

There was this door in front of me with this music coming out and people celebrating with utter joy that I knew and recognize[d] as home. Once [I] crossed, I couldn't come back.

I reached the point where I felt I had to make the choice whether to go back to life or onward into death. My best friend was there (who had died of cancer two years before), and she told me that this was as far as I could go or I would not be able to turn back. "You have come to the edge. This is as far as you can go," she said. "Now go back and live your life fully and fearlessly."

I wasn't allowed to cross that boundary. There was no choice.

The NDERF survey asked, "Did you reach a boundary or limiting physical structure?" To this question 31.0 percent of NDErs answered "Yes."

12. A Return to the Body, Either Voluntary or Involuntary

I remember as I looked down at them, I said to the angel, "Why don't they just let her die?" I did not realize, at that time, the body that I was looking at was mine. Then in a commanding voice, she [the angel] said, "You must go back now." . . . "She must live," she said in a soft calming voice. "She has a son to raise."

I was really hurt that I couldn't stay because there wasn't anything that I wanted more than to stay. Pure love is the best way to describe the being and place that I would be leaving. Under protest, I was sent back.

I found out that my purpose now would be to live "heaven on earth" using this new understanding, and also to share this knowledge with other people. However, I had the choice of whether to come back into life or go toward death. I was made to understand that it was not my time, but I always had the choice, and if I chose death, I would not be experiencing a lot of the gifts that the rest of my life still held in store. One of the things I wanted to know was that if I chose life, would I have to come back to this sick body, because my body was very, very sick and the organs had stopped functioning. I was then made to understand that if I chose life, my body would heal very quickly. I would see a difference in not months or weeks, but days!

The NDERF survey asked, "Were you involved in or aware of a decision regarding your return to the body?" To this question, 58.5 percent answered "Yes."

EXPERIENCE PROVIDES THE BEST EVIDENCE

As far as I'm concerned, it makes perfect sense that the best evidence for understanding what happens when we die would come from those who actually *did* nearly die or even experienced clinical death. This commonsense perspective is certainly validated in the NDERF study. The substantial majority of people who had a near-death experience believe their NDEs are real and are evidence of an afterlife. For NDErs, having a near-death experience is their personal proof of both the reality of the NDE *and* an afterlife.

In science, confirming the reality of a concept generally comes not from a single observation or study but from many independent studies with different methodologies. This cross-checking among scientific studies has always been the foundation for validating scientific discoveries. Thus it is vitally important to note that the NDERF study findings are corroborated by hundreds of prior NDE studies conducted by scores of NDE researchers. Throughout this book we cite many major NDE studies by other researchers. These other studies almost always make the same observations and come to the same conclusions as the NDERF study. This adds to the converging lines of evidence that lead me to conclude: *There is life after death.*

I know this belief takes me out on a limb. Despite a recent poll by the Pew Forum on Religion and Public Life that shows 74 percent of Americans believe in life after death, I also know that this belief is often attributed to people with deep religious conviction.[8] I want to make it clear that I am both a scientist *and* a believer in life after death.

I have reconsidered much of what I was taught in medical school. This reconsideration began many years ago, when NDERF had just started. I was in the medical library searching fruitlessly for information about near-death experiences. It was unusually quiet that day, and as I sat amid tens of thousands of books and journals, I easily became lost in my thoughts. At my fingertips were the greatest medical and scientific studies and concepts in the world. Yet as I searched them, I found that the answer to the mystery of near-death experiences was not here. In the collective knowledge around me from the world's greatest doctors and medical scientists, I could find precious little to help me fully understand the near-death experience.

I left the medical library with the question I had come in with: *What's the key to understanding near-death experiences?*

Later the answer came to me. It was so simple, yet it required a mind-set different from the one cultivated in my academic training. The answer: listen, and listen *carefully,* to the people who have gone through a near-death experience. They surely are one of the best sources for understanding what awaits us at the brink of death and beyond. Since realizing that fact, I have never looked back. Near-death studies focus on stories and the people who tell them. It is through these people and their stories that answers to many important questions about mortality may be found.

1

FIRST ENCOUNTERS

A man should look for what is, and not what he thinks should be.
—Albert Einstein

I was in my medical residency at the University of Iowa, looking for a particular article on cancer in the library. The article
I was seeking had been published in the *Journal of the American Medical Association* (*JAMA*), one of the world's most prestigious medical journals. The journal comes out weekly and
is a fascinating compilation of medical science and research.
It is almost impossible for me to pick up an issue and look at
only one article, and that is what happened on this day in
1984 when I sat down with issue number 244.

I began thumbing through the journal until I reached a
rebuttal to an article titled "To Sleep, Perchance to Dream,"
by Richard Blacher, MD, of Tufts University in Boston.[1] The
rebuttal was a letter written by Dr. Michael Sabom and was
simply titled "The Near-Death Experience."

What's this "near-death experience"? I thought. Medically speaking, I knew of no conscious experience that could take place near the point of death. Aren't people generally unconscious when they are near death? I wondered. Doesn't the very term *unconscious* imply that there is no possibility of an organized conscious experience?

Leaning forward in my chair, I began to read the letter that would change my life.

Blacher had rattled Sabom with a comment about near-death experiences, saying that they tell us nothing of the final state of death itself. Blacher went on to insist that misinterpretation of this experience could be avoided with a closer examination of this phenomenon, which is what Sabom had recently done. Sabom's response to Blacher's article had some electricity running through it.

I have recently conducted a systematic investigation of these experiences in 107 persons known to have survived an episode of unconsciousness and near death (i.e., cardiac arrest and coma). Using standardized interview techniques, the social, religious and demographic backgrounds of each person were evaluated along with the details of each medical crisis event and any possible recollections from the period of unconsciousness. . . .

. . . I have had patients describe extensive "out of body" experiences during open heart surgery in which they observed the operation in distinct "visual" detail.

To date, I have been unable to find an adequate medical explanation for the NDE. Blacher suggests that these experiences represent a "fantasy of death" and are manifestations of a hypoxic brain attempting to deal with "the anxieties provoked by medical procedures and talk." Experimentally, persons subjected to severe hypoxia have consistently reported having a confused and muddled memory with severe perceptual impairment preceding the loss of consciousness. This differs from the clear "visual" perception of ongoing physical events following loss of consciousness as found in the NDE. Moreover, many NDEs have occurred in settings far removed from "the anxieties provoked by medical procedures and talk."

Blacher points out that "the physicians must be especially wary of accepting religious belief as scientific data." I might add that equal caution should be exercised in accepting scientific belief as scientific data.[2]

After reading Sabom's response I was stunned. Even though Sabom had written only a brief letter to the editor, that letter addressed an aspect of medicine that was entirely new to me. Near-death experiences! Nothing in my medical training had prepared me for a discussion of the topic. It was as though I had missed a vital class and had now found some study material to begin filling that gap in my education.

I asked myself, Why isn't there more research on this phenomenon? I remember sitting for some time in the library thinking about what I had just read. Then the sound of a book being closed brought me back to the present. I was studying to become a radiation oncologist—a physician who uses radiation to treat cancer—and I couldn't let myself get sidetracked, even for an afternoon.

I put the subject of near-death experiences out of my head and went on with my medical studies.

Or at least I *tried* to go on as if nothing had happened. After my chance encounter with Sabom's letter in *JAMA,* it seemed as though near-death experiences sprang up everywhere. I read about them in magazines and newspapers and watched them on television as people told remarkable stories of leaving their bodies at the point of death and going to another world.

I read the classic works on near-death experiences and found a wide variety of definitions for this experience. The term *near-death experience* was coined by Dr. Raymond Moody in his bestselling book, *Life After Life,* a work about the first widely known study of NDEs.[3] Dr. Moody first defined *near-death experience* in 1977 to mean "any conscious perceptual experience which takes place during . . . an event in which a person could very easily die or be killed (and even may be so close as to be believed or pronounced clinically dead) but nonetheless survives, and continues physical life."[4]

Over a decade later Moody redefined *near-death experience* as "profound spiritual events that happen, uninvited, to some individuals at the point of death."[5]

Regardless of the exact definition, the question that stuck in my mind was: How is it that people who are clinically dead or nearly so can have these highly lucid experiences? For example, in Moody's book *The Light Beyond,* a woman's heart stops on the operating table as anesthetic is being administered, due to an allergic reaction.

Rather than having no awareness of her surroundings, as the notion of death would lead me to assume, she told Dr. Moody that she became "relaxed and at peace." Then a highly lucid series of events began to unfold. Here in her own words is her NDE:

I found myself floating up toward the ceiling. I could see everyone around the bed very plainly, even my own body. I thought how odd it was that they were upset about my body. I was fine and I wanted them to know that, but there seemed to be no way to let them know. It was as though there were a veil or a screen between me and the others in the room.

I became aware of an opening, if I can call it that. It appeared to be elongated and dark, and I began to zoom through it. I was puzzled yet exhilarated. I came out of this tunnel into a realm of soft, brilliant love and light. The love was everywhere. It surrounded me and seemed to soak through into my very being. At some point I was shown, or saw, the events of my life. They were in a kind of vast panorama. All of this is really just indescribable. People I knew who had died were there with me in the light—a friend who had died in college, my grandfather, and a great-aunt, among others. They were happy, beaming.

I didn't want to go back, but I was told that I had to by a man in light. I was being told that I had not completed what I had to do in life.

I came back into my body with a sudden lurch.[6]

This was an experience that happened to someone whose heart had stopped! How could that be? After all, *death,* simply defined (according to Merriam-Webster Online), is "a permanent cessation of all vital functions—the end of life." Yet I was reading dozens of case studies in which people whose hearts had stopped and who were in an unconscious state recounted lucid events containing elements that were remarkably similar to one another.

ASTOUNDING STORY

I was impressed by the work of Moody and many other early NDE researchers but still very surprised at the lack of even more extensive research. After all, isn't humankind's most sought after answer the one to the question *Do we survive bodily death?* I began to wonder if I myself should become involved in researching these fascinating, seemingly other-world journeys.

Then something happened that helped me decide.

A friend of mine from undergraduate days returned to Iowa for a visit, and we got together for dinner so I could meet his new wife. Before long, my friend's wife began to talk about her allergies, which turned out to be varied and quite severe—so severe, in fact, that at one point she had a severe allergic reaction while under general anesthesia and "coded" on the operating table.

As she talked about her heart stopping, she had no fear in her voice, just a sense of wonder. I decided to probe a little.

"That's odd," I said. "I have heard my patients talk about facing death, but not with that tone of voice."

The table fell silent. It was clear that I had stumbled onto something. I looked around and struggled to ask the question that was on my mind.

"Did anything happen to you when you coded on that table?" I asked.

Her immediate and emphatic response was "Why, yes!" And right there, in this dimly lit restaurant on a frigid winter's night in Iowa City, I heard my first in-person near-death experience.

Sheila's NDE

I have always suffered from multiple allergies.[7] This was merely a lifelong nuisance until that fateful day that my allergies became a much greater threat to my life. I told the surgeon and anesthesiologist about all my allergies. This was elective surgery and not an emergency. In spite of the medical team doing everything they could, I had a severe allergic reaction to a medication during the operation. This allergic reaction was so severe that my heart stopped.

Immediately after my heart stopped I found myself at ceiling level. I could see the EKG machine I was hooked to. The EKG was flatlined. The doctors and nurses were frantically trying to bring me back to life. The scene below me was a near-panic situation. In contrast to the chaos below, I felt a profound sense of peace. I was completely free of any pain. My consciousness drifted out of the operating room and moved into a nursing station. I immediately recognized that this was the nursing station on the floor where I had been prior to my surgery. From my vantage point near the ceiling, I saw the nurses bustling about performing their daily duties.

After I watched the nurses a while, a tunnel opened up. I was drawn to the tunnel. I then passed through the tunnel and became aware of a bright light at the end of the tunnel. I felt peaceful. After I passed through the tunnel, I found myself in an area of beautiful, mystical light. In front of me were several of my beloved relatives who had previously died. It was a joyous reunion, and we embraced.

I found myself with a mystical being of overwhelming love and compassion. "Do you want to go back?" I was asked. I responded, "I don't know," which was just like my old indecisive self at the time. After further discussion, I knew the choice to return to my physical body was mine. It was a most difficult decision. I was in a realm of overwhelming love. In this realm I knew I was truly home. Finally, I returned to my body.

I awoke in the ICU over a day later. I had tubes and wires all over me. I could not talk about my profound experience. Later I returned to the floor of the hospital where I had been before surgery. Here was the nursing station I visited during my NDE. I finally worked up the courage to share what I saw during my NDE with one of the nurses. The nurse responded with a look of shock and fright. This was a Catholic hospital. Not surprisingly, a nun was sent to talk with me. I patiently explained all that I had experienced. The nun listened carefully and then declared my experience to be the "work of the devil." You can understand my enormous reluctance to share my NDE with anyone after this.

When Sheila finished her story, there was silence around the table for some time. I don't remember eating any more of my meal although I may have. I do remember being so astonished by the story that I fell silent as the evening wore on. What I had just heard was the most dramatic story that had ever been shared with me. Every instinct I had as a human being and a physician told me that this experience was absolutely real. In those moments my perception of the world was completely changed. I remember thinking these experiences could change my views about life, death, God, and the world we live in.

I left the restaurant that night determined to begin my own research on near-death experiences. I later devised ambitious plans to collect hundreds of near-death experience case studies and scientifically study them, to determine conclusively for myself if NDEs were reality or just phantasms of the brain.

My studies would not happen for another ten years.

JOURNEY TOWARD UNDERSTANDING

Build it and they will come.
—W. P. Kinsella, *Field of Dreams*

The year was 1998, and I was now in Las Vegas practicing the medical specialty of radiation oncology. The nineties was the decade in which the Internet exploded. Everyone was rapidly becoming smitten with this big brain in the sky, and I was no different.

Despite the steep learning curve of building websites with primitive software and slow connections, I had decided in 1997 to build the *Radiation Oncology Online Journal* (ROOJ.com) as a way of sharing credible information about this medical specialty with the world. It took a tremendous amount of time and effort outside of my clinical practice to assemble this nonprofit website, which I maintain as a way of providing solid information to the public about cancer treatment.

By the time I completed the ROOJ site I was an expert in website computer code. Then the idea hit me: build a website that will collect near-death experience case studies. By doing this I could amass a large number of NDE stories from around the world. Working with a large number of NDEs is important because medical studies involving a large study group produce more reliable results than do those studying a small group of people.

I built on the curiosity and work of those who had gone before me. Over the ten years since I heard Sheila recount her personal story, I had stayed in close contact with research in the field of near-death studies. Hundreds of scholarly articles had been written on near-death experience, including publications in many of the world's most prestigious medical and scientific journals. I read the works of many major NDE researchers, including those of Dr. Moody; Melvin Morse, MD; Bruce Greyson, MD; Michael Sabom, MD; and Ken Ring, PhD. I also found myself fascinated with some of the individual stories, like that of Betty Eadie (*Embraced by the Light*[1]). All of these books relied heavily on case studies. These stories of individual NDErs fed the sense of mystery I associated with this subject.

Now I was even more interested in searching for the truth than I had been ten years earlier. The implications of these experiences were so profound that I wanted to research the subject to determine if they were truly real.

The Internet was an ideal way to carry out this research. Through a website, I could reach people around the world who were willing to share their near-death experience with others. They weren't being paid to write about their experience and had no intention of appearing on television. They would simply tell their stories directly in their own words. I would offer a series of questions aimed at helping NDErs fully express and deeply explore their incredible experience. There would be no interviewer present to possibly guide the answers or encourage embellishment, and no time constraints. Reading their shared stories would be like reading the most intimate of diary pages. By collecting NDEs via the Internet, I could examine the content of a large number of experiences, reliably determining similarities and differences, and find out once and for all if NDEs are real or imagined.

In the past a considerable amount of research had been accomplished but often with only a few NDEs. This wasn't the fault of the researchers. Case studies of NDEs are not easy to find. Although some research indicates that as much as 5 percent of the U.S. population has had a near-death experience, many people keep them secret or find no reason to entrust their most intimate spiritual experience with their doctor or researchers.[2]

An unfortunate reason NDErs might not share their stories is the attitude of many in medicine toward these experiences. I have heard many heartbreaking stories from NDErs who shared highly accurate observations of their own resuscitations, only to have physicians dismiss their experiences as insignificant. Even though there is no reason NDErs should have any conscious awareness of their resuscitation, their accounts were given short shrift by physicians who should have marveled at their patients' experiences rather than ridiculed them.

I spent many years serving on the board of directors of the International Association for Near-Death Studies. During our meetings I heard far too many stories of the problems

NDErs encountered when they tried to tell their near-death experiences to the medical staff. One of the classic stories was a patient who told his doctor about his NDE in front of several nurses. When the patient finished telling his story, the doctor looked up from his clipboard and said, "Don't think too much about it. It was just fantasy."

When the doctor left the room, the nurses closed in around the crushed patient and said, "It's not fantasy. We hear about these events all the time from patients. Doctors like him live in fantasy. They never hear these because they don't listen to their patients."

This was one way in which taking case studies over the Internet was superior to interviewing people directly. People who have these intimate experiences are sometimes reluctant to be interviewed in person and in a formal way about their NDE. They may feel that the interviewer isn't sincerely interested in their experience, or they may feel awkward about sharing such an unworldly experience with others.

Responding to an Internet survey, by contrast, offers the NDEr a chance to share these remarkable events as if they are talking to themselves. Rather than being forced to overcome any discomfort they might have with an interviewer, they are comfortably recounting their own story privately, by themselves. They also can take as much time as they want. Many NDErs shared their appreciation with me after they took the survey. They found the survey helped them to accurately and comprehensively convey their experience.

This is why I felt (and still do) that an Internet survey is more effective in many ways than a face-to-face interview.

Of course, I had concerns as I put together the NDE website survey. For example, how could I tell for certain if the stories being told were valid? I pondered this question a lot and decided to rely on the tried-and-true scientific method of redundancy. Redundancy in interviewing means asking the same question (or questions that revolve around the same concept) several times in slightly different ways. For instance, in the demographic portion of the questionnaire, there is a box to check if the person had an out-of-body experience. One would expect that if this box was checked, then the answer to the question "Did you experience a separation of your consciousness from your body?" should be "Yes." If we find inconsistencies in a person's answers, we can check the narrative to see what the NDEr really experienced. Later, after large numbers of NDEs were shared, I was impressed at how consistent the responses were to the redundant questions.

The NDERF Internet survey reaches NDErs who have never shared their near-death experience with another person and would be unlikely to be reached by any other methodology used to study NDEs. The NDERF survey asks, "Have you shared this experience with others?" To this question, 8.5 percent of NDErs answered "No."

Importantly, many studies have directly compared the reliability of Internet surveys with the more traditional pencil-and-paper surveys by studying groups of people who took surveys with both methods. The consensus of these studies is that an Internet survey is as reliable as the pencil-and-paper survey method. This further validates the reliability of the NDERF survey.[3]

I already knew I needed to listen carefully to the near-death experiencers, so it made sense to ask the NDErs themselves how accurate they thought the NDERF survey was. Near the end of the current website survey, I ask an important question: "Did the questions asked and information you provided so far accurately and comprehensively describe your experience?" Of 613 NDErs responding, the answers were 84.5 percent "Yes," 8.8 percent "Uncertain," and only 6.7 percent "No." This is some of the strongest possible validation of the reliability of the NDERF Internet survey, from the NDErs themselves.

Finally, my background as a physician helps me determine if a life-threatening event actually happened. I use the Karnofsky scale, which is a medical scale widely used to measure closeness to death. Karnofsky scores range from 100 (no physical compromise) to 10 (moribund) to 0 (clinically dead).[4] I can also determine if the medical events described in the NDEs are medically plausible.

In the early days of the website, I was concerned there might be frauds or pranksters claiming to have had a near-death experience. I am glad to say this is very rare. For one thing, there is no incentive—financial or otherwise—to spend a substantial amount of time filling out the lengthy and complex survey form in order to claim a false NDE. Eventually, those trying to submit a falsified NDE discover how difficult it is to respond to a detailed survey if they have never had such an experience. In over ten years, we have uncovered fewer than ten clearly fraudulent accounts submitted on the NDERF survey form and have removed them promptly from the website and database.

I was also concerned that there might be copycat accounts, in which all or part of an NDE would be copied or plagiarized from another source. This has happened, but again very rarely. When it does, readers of the website report the copycat account, and we remove it from the site. The enormous number of visitors to the NDERF website helps assure that none of the posted NDEs are plagiarized.

I had other concerns too. Near-death experiences are complex and might be difficult for some to express in words. This is why many researchers in the past have considered them to be "ineffable," or incapable of being expressed in words. It is not uncommon to hear an NDEr describe their experience as being, well, *indescribable*. I was concerned that many people might find it impossible to express what happened.

Are NDEs generally ineffable? I asked myself as I assembled the questionnaire for the NDERF site.

Given all these concerns, was I wasting my time?

The website for the Near Death Experience Research Foundation (NDERF, www.nderf.org) was launched on the World Wide Web on August 30, 1998. I had many questions about whether the NDERF site would be successful. Was the questionnaire too long? Did NDErs really want to share their experience with the world?[5] Would people trust a site like this?

I had not spent money on publicity for the site. Several months later, by monitoring the Web traffic, I could tell that the site had been visited by relatively few. Our search engine ranking was a pitiful 64.

Had I wasted hundreds of hours to accomplish nothing? Would enough experiences ever be shared with NDERF to answer my questions about the reality of NDEs?

Humbled, I continued to work diligently on the site. By now I had told several friends about the site and shared my concerns that few people were actually visiting it, let alone filling out the questionnaire. When I said this, some of my friends would simply smile and utter one of the most popular movie lines in history: "If you build it, they will come." This is the classic line from the film *Field of Dreams,* in which an Iowa farmer builds a baseball field on his farm in hopes that several long-dead baseball players will come there to play.

As you can imagine, "build it and they will come" is not the creed of evidence-based medicine. We like to start with a little more science than that. As a result, I still cringe a little whenever I hear this Hollywood aphorism. However, I continued to build the site in hopes that, yes, they would come.

And finally, come they did. By December 1998 I downloaded the first twenty-two case studies from the website with great anticipation. I was jubilant. With all the effort I had put into the site, I was now going to have information about NDEs from the source—people who had the experiences! As a scientist and a "prove it to me" kind of man, I personally needed precisely this kind of information to begin to scientifically study NDEs.

Those first twenty-two case studies didn't disappoint. As I read them it started to become obvious to me that the NDEs were real. I could see the same pattern of elements that Dr. Moody and other researchers had outlined in their work, including such elements as consciousness occurring apart from the body at the time of a life-threatening event.

Reading these early case studies was exciting beyond my wildest dreams. It became clear to me that by studying a large number of these NDEs in words that came directly from those who had experienced them, I could hope to eventually provide some answers to humankind's most perplexing question: What happens when we die?

Below are paraphrases[6] of two of the first twenty-two NDE case studies I was honored to receive on the NDERF website:

Experience #16: "I Felt Like a Fly on the Wall"

In 1963 this young man lost control of his car and collided with a brick wall. His injuries were severe enough to fracture his face and sinus cavities and to break his jaw. Badly hurt, he sat on wet grass near the destroyed vehicle and then drifted into unconsciousness. As you read this, note the calmness with which he describes his experience as well as the presence of a very powerful out-of-body experience that seemed to indicate to him that all would be well in his life despite this near-fatal accident. Here's his story:

I was in a severe automobile accident several years ago. The steering wheel smashed my face. The accident happened in a rainstorm, and I ran off the road and hit a brick wall.

For a while after the crash I felt nothing, and then the pain started to burn in my face. I got out of the car and lay down, hoping it would make me feel better, but it didn't. Finally I just blacked out. When I awoke, I couldn't see anything because my face was covered, but I could tell I was in a hospital from the sounds and the fact that I was on some kind of bed.

I don't know how long it was, but I had the distinct sensation that I was floating out of my body. I saw my parents, who were there at the bedside, and could feel their emotional pain. It was strange. I should have been in pain but wasn't. Instead I was standing next to my parents trying to console them as they looked at their darling son, whom they had just been told was going to die. It was horrific, but there was nothing I could do about it. I stood next to my mother and tried to get her attention, but I couldn't because she didn't know I was there. I looked at my own body but wasn't interested in what I was seeing. I actually felt like a fly on the wall.

Something in my mind finally clicked as I realized that they would eventually discover that I was not in pain, whether it was here on earth or not. At that point my empathetic pain went away and I focused on my experience. I remember thinking, "So this is what death is about," as I rose further out of my body.

A light came into view and became larger and brighter as I drew closer. I knew this was it, the end of my life, and I wasn't afraid. But as I drew near, a voice shouted at me to stop. And I mean shouted. "No, not yet!" the voice said.

When that happened I felt myself return very hard into my body. I gasped very loudly, but I knew I was going to survive after that. When they say it's not your time, it's not your time.

When I first read this man's account of his near-fatal automobile accident, I was taken by the calmness with which he described the sense of peace and painlessness that came over him in the hospital. I was also intrigued by his description of the light that formed the boundary between life and death, as well as the strong voice that stopped him from crossing into the light.

This man came back from his experience with the ability to "intuit people's feelings" (his words) as well as understand their emotional logic. *Intuiting people's feelings* may be one type of psychic experience. I would encounter many more NDEs describing psychic experiences in the future.

Experience #21: "Wake Up, Diane"

Diane had an unusual problem. When she sat on the couch in the afternoon to watch her favorite soap opera, the young woman found herself falling asleep and having great difficulty waking up. The problem disturbed her so much that she mentioned it to her husband, who could offer no solution. Finally she decided to sit up on the sofa and watch the program rather than lie down. As it turned out, sitting up made the problem worse. Behind her, about five feet from the couch, was a leaking gas pipe that emitted enough natural gas into the room to nearly kill her. Ironically, she would have died had it not been for a visitation by her deceased grandmother during her NDE that brought her back. Here is a paraphrase of her story:

I sat myself down on the couch and started watching my favorite soap opera, and next thing I knew someone was yelling at me to wake up. I kept hearing this voice telling me to "wake up, Diane, you have to wake up."

When Diane opened her eyes, she was looking at her grandmother who had died when she was only three years old. The grandmother smiled and told Diane to get up and follow her to safety. When she got up to follow, Diane realized she had left her body, which was now below her on the sofa. She felt no fear as she looked down at her body. She also felt no fear at the realization that there were two spirits elevated with her, one on either side of her spiritual body.

While out of her body she felt a sense of enormous peace and love. One of the spirits told her she could either stay in her spiritual body or return to the physical body below. It was a tough decision for Diane, but one that led to her choosing the physical body because she still had things left to do on earth. With the making of that choice, Diane took a deep and painful breath, and then another, until she awoke and realized that she had nearly been asphyxiated by the gas leak.

Needless to say, the gas leak was fixed soon after Diane's NDE. The experience, however, had a lasting effect on her life. Here is a paraphrase of what Diane wrote:

The experience taught me that everything is known. At the time, I did not feel it was important to ask anything. God has made it so we will know everything when we die.

WORLDWIDE PARTICIPATION

These twenty-two case reports were the first in what would be an explosion of global participation on the NDERF website. In the decade since NDERF began, readers have sent hundreds of e-mails expressing gratitude for how meaningful the stories are to them. I have received e-mails from cancer patients and people with other serious illnesses who take great comfort in coming to the same conclusion as I, that life continues after bodily death.

Ultimately, NDEs in more than twenty languages have been shared with NDERF. Before I knew it, readers from more than 110 countries were devouring more than 300,000 page views per month on the NDERF website.

At first I considered the variety of languages to be a problem. The NDEs that were sent from people in other countries in languages other than English had to be translated into English, and online translation engines didn't do it very well. I barely had time to analyze the experiences that people had entered in English, let alone find translators.

Then Jody, longtime webmaster of NDERF, came to the rescue. She is an attorney who is just as interested in spiritual matters as in those of jurisprudence. We met shortly before I moved to Tacoma, Washington, in the year 2000. When we first met, I could tell that she had a very strong spiritual side and that she was intrigued by the work I was doing in near-death experiences. She was unfamiliar with NDEs but became more and more fascinated with them as I told her about the case studies that were now streaming in. Even with her discernment as a lawyer, she was taken by the consistency of the experiences.

"This is amazing," she said one day. "And it's all for real."

One of the things she had become interested in was whether NDEs were the same from culture to culture. And if so, could the commonality of the NDEs in different cultures create a bridge of world peace? By having access to NDEs written by people in other countries, she realized she could answer her questions firsthand. The quest for knowledge drove Jody to go on a Web search for translators. Over time she found over 250 volunteers willing to translate the multitude of languages spoken in the world. With Jody's diligent assistance, the NDERF site is by far the largest publicly accessible collection of both English and non-English NDEs in the world.

The near-death experiences on NDERF are edited only to correct spelling and obvious grammar errors, remove information that would identify specific individuals, and take out grossly disparaging remarks about specific institutions. Other than those insignificant changes, the NDEs you read on the site are the highly charged experiences written by the NDErs themselves.

WHAT WE FOUND

By studying thousands of detailed accounts of NDErs, I found the evidence that led to this astounding conclusion: *NDEs provide such powerful scientific evidence that it is reasonable to accept the existence of an afterlife.*

Yes, you read that correctly. I have studied thousands of near-death experiences. I have carefully considered the evidence NDEs present regarding the existence of an afterlife. I believe without a shadow of a doubt that there is life after physical death.

My research convinces me that near-death experiences are the exit from this life and the entrance to another life. As one NDEr declared, "I saw these vivid colors of what I believe to be crystal, and the overwhelming feeling of knowing there *is* an afterlife and it is good [makes me have] no fear of death whatsoever!"

This book presents the remarkable results of the largest scientific NDE study ever reported using this methodology. In the NDERF study we examined the content of more than 1,300 NDEs. Previous scientific NDE studies generally examined only a few hundred case studies at most. With great care, we analyzed the twelve elements of the near-death experience. By looking deeply at the accounts of these NDErs, we have found some answers to humankind's oldest and deepest questions about the afterlife.

In my work as a radiation oncologist, my life is built around science. It couldn't be any other way. I deliver precision doses of radiation to kill cancerous tumors. There are few other forms of medical science that require such precision. I love what I do and have carried this love of science to other parts of my life. The data and conclusions you read here are based on the scientific principles that I adhere to.

I would be remiss if I didn't say that my scientific conclusions have greatly affected my level of compassion. Sometimes frightened cancer patients familiar with my NDE research will ask me what will happen when they die. If they ask, I confidently present to them the evidence of the afterlife that I have accumulated through a decade of dedicated research. I believe that what I share with these cancer patients helps them to better face their life-threatening illness with increased courage and hope.

By reviewing the findings of the NDERF study, I have derived nine lines of reasoning that—to my mind—prove the existence of life after death. Below are those lines of evidence, each with its own brief commentary. In the remaining chapters of this book, I will examine each of the lines of evidence in depth so you can see why I came to the conclusion I did: It is reasonable to accept the existence of an afterlife.

EVIDENCE OF THE AFTERLIFE

1. It is medically inexplicable to have a highly organized and lucid experience while unconscious or clinically dead. In our NDERF research, *near death* is defined as an individual who is physically compromised to the extent that death would be expected unless their physical condition improves. Those who are near death are generally unconscious and may be clinically dead with loss of breathing and heartbeat.

To understand how remarkable it is to have a conscious experience at a time of clinical death, it is helpful to understand that when the heart stops beating, blood immediately stops flowing to the brain. Approximately ten to twenty seconds after blood stops flowing to the brain, brain activity necessary for consciousness stops. Brain activity can be measured by an electroencephalogram (EEG), which measures brain electrical activity. When brain activity stops, the EEG readings go flat, indicating no measurable brain electrical activity.

Medically, I can't conceive of any meaningful experience that could occur near death. Aren't people near death generally unconscious? Doesn't the very term *unconscious* mean that there is no possibility of an organized conscious experience? Yet despite what should be a blank slate for NDErs, they describe highly lucid, organized, and real experiences. In fact, NDErs say they are usually experiencing a more heightened state of awareness than in everyday earthly life. This is medically inexplicable given that NDEs generally occur during unconsciousness.

2. NDErs may see and hear in the out-of-body (OBE) state, and what they perceive is nearly always real. An out-of-body experience (OBE) is the first element of the experience for many NDErs. During the OBE, many NDErs describe events that they shouldn't be able to see, mainly because they are unconscious or because the events are taking place somewhere else, far away from their body. Events often include seeing their own unconscious body as well as frantic resuscitation efforts to revive them. These observations have been verified as realistic in hundreds of reports.

3. *NDEs occur during general anesthesia when no form of consciousness should be taking place.* While under general anesthesia, it should be impossible to have a lucid experience, let alone one of greater consciousness than everyday life. The NDERF survey has yielded dozens of NDEs that took place under general anesthesia. Here is one such incident that happened to Debora. At the age of thirteen she went into the hospital for minor surgery, and the anesthetic caused her heart to stop. As her doctor struggled to keep her alive, Debora suddenly found herself out of her body:

My heart stopped from anesthesia during surgery. . . . I floated up to the ceiling and could see my body lying on the table. The doctors were alarmed and saying that they were losing me. I was not scared; I was with a couple of very kind people that I believed at the time were angels. They told me not to worry; they would take care of me. I heard a whooshing sound and was being propelled up through a dark tunnel toward a light. . . . A woman held out her hand to me; she was lovely, and I felt that she loved me and knew who I was. I felt safe in her company. I didn't know who she was. . . . One day a few years after the surgery my mother showed me a picture of my paternal grandmother, who had died giving birth to my father. It was the lovely woman who held my hand at the other side of the tunnel. I had never seen a picture of her before.

4. *NDEs take place among those who are blind, and these NDEs often include visual experiences.* Individuals totally blind from birth are completely unable to perceive the visual world that the rest of us do in everyday life. To those born blind, the ability to see is an abstract concept. They understand the world only from their senses of hearing, touch, taste, and smell. Their dreams do not include vision, although they may include other senses such as sound and touch. Vision cannot be adequately explained to a person blind from birth by drawing analogies to the four remaining senses they possess. Yet when a blind person has an NDE, the experience usually includes vision.

5. *A life review during the NDE accurately reflects real events in the NDEr's life, even if those events have been forgotten.* A life review involves a review of prior events in the NDEr's life. Fragments of the person's earthly life may be seen, or the review may be fully panoramic with a comprehensive review of most of the prior life. Here is one such example, from a young woman from India who nearly died from a complication of anesthesia:

My entire consciousness seemed to be in my head. Then I started seeing pictures. I think they were in color. It was as if someone had started a movie of myself and of my entire life, but going backwards from the present moment. The pictures were about my family, my mother, other members, others, and it seemed that the most meaningful, loving, caring relationships were being focused upon. I could sense the real meaning of these rela-

tionships. I had a sense of love and gratitude towards the persons appearing in my flashback. This panoramic review of my life was very distinct; every little detail of the incidents, relationships, was there—the relationships in some sort of distilled essence of meaning. The review was measured in the beginning, but then the pictures came in faster and faster, and [it] seemed like the movie reel was running out. . . . It went faster and faster, and then I heard myself, along with the entire universe in my head, screaming in a crescendo, "Allah ho akbar!" (God is great).

6. *Virtually all beings encountered during NDEs are deceased at the time of the NDE, and most are deceased relatives.* When NDErs encounter people that they knew from their earthly life, those people are almost always deceased at the time of the NDE. By contrast, in dreams or hallucinations the beings encountered are much more likely to be living. This is another distinguishing feature between NDEs and dreams or hallucinations, further suggesting the reality of NDEs.

Many times the NDErs encounter a being that seems familiar, but his or her identity is unknown. The NDEr may later discover the identity of this familiar but unknown being, for instance by looking at old family photographs.

7. *The striking similarity of content in NDEs among very young children and that of adults strongly suggests that the content of NDEs is not due to preexisting beliefs.* Children—even those under the age of six—have virtually the same elements in their near-death experiences as adults do. This is strong evidence in itself that near-death experiences are real, not dreams or fabrications. Why? Because very young children almost certainly have never heard of near-death experiences, as adults often have. They probably don't know

anything about life reviews, tunnel experiences, out-of-body experiences, or any of the other elements of the NDE. They become aware of such things, usually for the first time, when the experience actually happens.

The fact that children have virtually the same elements of near-death experiences that adults do makes this one of the most convincing lines of evidence that NDEs are real events and not due to preexisting beliefs, cultural influences, or prior life experiences.

8. The remarkable consistency of NDEs around the world is evidence that NDEs are real events. There is a simple analogy I like to use that illustrates this point: If families from the United States, Spain, and Mexico all go to Paris, do they see the same Eiffel Tower? The answer, of course, is yes. The only difference might be in the way the different cultures describe this landmark. The same is true of people from different cultures who have near-death experiences. Our collection of NDEs from cultures worldwide shows striking similarity in content among all of them.

9. NDErs are transformed in many ways by their experience, often for life. The NDERF study found consistent and long-lasting changes following NDEs. Near-death experiencers have a decreased fear of death, which seems to go hand in hand with an increased belief in the afterlife. In addition, NDErs become more loving and compassionate in their interaction with other people. Our study found that near-death experiencers may seek out helping or healing professions after their brush with death. Also, many NDErs in the study had been changed so much by their experience that they were no longer the same; they had become nicer!

The NDERF study also found that 45.0 percent of those surveyed said they had "psychic, paranormal, or other special gifts" that they did not have prior to the experience. They went on to provide many such experiences in the narrative portion of their survey. One such story of supernatural gifts came from Thomas, who nearly died from a heart rhythm irregularity. What he had to say about his extraordinary gifts was short and to the point:

I felt a need to meditate. Upon doing so I was able to hear voices and see things. (Some might call [them] spirits or unearthly beings.) I have the ability to see auras; I sense other people's pain and am able to heal with touch. For a while I had brief spurts of telekinesis.

One of the most intriguing—to me—transformations were the unexpected healings that some reported. We have encountered many such cases in the NDERF study, including ones in which people with very serious illnesses, both physical and mental, believe they were healed around the time of their NDEs.

The transformational qualities of the NDE give me reason to believe that whatever a person experiences on the other side, a little bit of it may come back, bringing change here as well.

STRONG AND BOLD PROOF

Any one of these lines of evidence on its own strongly suggests an afterlife. However, I consider the combination of these nine lines of evidence to be proof beyond a reasonable doubt of the existence of an afterlife. That is certainly a bold statement but one I am compelled to make after years of painstaking research.

An important NDERF survey question asks 613 NDErs what they think of the reality of their experience—how they viewed the reality of their experience shortly after its occurrence and also at the time they completed the survey. In response, 95.8 percent believed at the time of completing the survey that their NDE was definitely real. Not one NDEr said that the experience they had was "definitely not real."

And then there is the spiritual content of NDEs, namely answers to such age-old questions as: Why are we here on earth? What is important about our earthly existence? Is there an afterlife? Now that I have reviewed thousands of NDE case studies, I can say that the content of NDEs has substantial consistency in these answers. I would emphasize that this consistency tells us that something real is taking place in these NDEs. This remarkable consistency of spiritual messages suggests something extremely important, not only for the person near death, but for all of us.

The true strength of the NDERF study has been the sheer number of case studies we have examined and the consistency of results. From this volume and the consistency of their content and message, I believe we have some answers to humankind's most perplexing question: What happens when we die?

But that is my belief. The results of our groundbreaking research are presented in the following chapters. You be the judge.

PROOF #1: LUCID DEATH

For death begins with life's first breath,
and life begins at touch of death.
—John Oxenham

*Speaking both medically and logically, it is not possible to have
a highly lucid experience while unconscious or clinically dead.*

After all, being clinically dead means no longer having
the perceptions or senses of a living person. If this statement
is indeed true, then how do you explain events like the ones
in the following three NDEs? In each of these events—
cardiac arrest, brain hemorrhage, and a shooting—the person had a very lucid experience, which defies the fact that
she or he was unconscious and near death.

This first story is from a physician who worked feverishly
to revive an elderly patient. As you can see in his account
below, the patient appreciated the doctor's work from a ring-
side seat:

After twenty-eight shocks (I think), I got her back. She was technically without a cardiac rhythm of her own for 1.5 hours. . . . That night I went to the ICU and asked the elderly patient if she "remembered anything."

"Yes," she said, "I was in the corner of the room—floating—and saw you working on me. You shocked me, and I was dead. I saw a massively white bright light, and there were two angels there . . . telling me it wasn't my time and to go back. But I didn't want to."

This patient had a brain hemorrhage that dropped him to the ground. He said he could see "360 degrees" around his body. Before long, he had a profound sense of being dead, which wasn't a bad thing, by his account:

When I realized I was dead, which took several minutes, a great warmth of love engulfed me, and I felt arms wrap around me even though I had no physical form; colors were electric, smells fantastic. . . . I was also aware of the overpowering secret to life in its truly simple form and felt and believed that nothing else is real but the feeling. The experience of death has been the most real and physical experience of my life, and the world here felt cold and heavy and unreal for sometime afterward.

This patient was in a coma for three days, during which time he was visited by friends and family members. Still, he insisted he was out of body for the entire time and could hear and see what people in his room were doing. In one case he proved it. A woman had brought a lavender candle to the hospital and placed it in the drawer near his bed. When he came out of the coma, he knew which drawer the candle was in.

Not to go too far afield here, but the man also had prophetic dreams of a personal and worldwide nature. Not only did he "see" a relationship in his future as well as events in his child's future, but he also "saw" a world economic downturn and a nuclear explosion in North Korea.

Another example of lucid death comes from Michelle, who was shot by her boyfriend near Boston. She was in the process of breaking up with her beau and was in his basement apartment when she heard a loud blast and felt a hot, piercing pain in the back of her neck. As her mouth filled with blood, the boyfriend grabbed Michelle and said, "What have I done?"

She left her body, and from a spot in the corner of the room she watched as firefighters and police officers stepped around her body as they tried to figure out exactly what to do. The boyfriend's brother began to cry, and as he did he threw up on a police officer, which was a sight that made her laugh. It was then that she had this revelation about death:

I felt so blissful and whole . . . full of the most love I had ever experienced. I thought to myself, "If this is dying, then it's not as bad as everyone thinks it is." Then I saw a light from above me. It was pulling me away from the room. I figured it was okay to just let this happen, to go with the flow and accept whatever was to be. The light was getting brighter, engulfing my body. . . . Body? I had no body. It stayed back down in that damp room. I realized that I was dead physically but mentally I was still alive. My soul was now my "body." I looked up into the light. I could see someone beckoning me to come. He was there at the end of this lit tunnel. Then I heard a voice. It was a man's voice. He asked me if I was ready. I felt so good. It was so easy.

Millions of NDEs like these happen worldwide every year to people who are unconscious and may be clinically dead with a loss of breathing and heartbeat. Yet they are still having highly lucid experiences at the time of death, experiences that are clear, logical, and well structured.

Even more remarkable is an NDERF research finding that consciousness and alertness is usually *greater* during the NDE than everyday consciousness and alertness!

The NDERF survey asked, "How did your highest level of consciousness and alertness during the experience compare to your normal, everyday consciousness and alertness?" Of 613 NDErs surveyed, 74.4 percent indicated they had "More consciousness and alertness than normal"; 19.9 percent experienced "Normal consciousness and alertness"; and only 5.7 percent had "Less consciousness and alertness than normal."

The concept of a higher level of consciousness and alertness is subjective, so the NDERF survey asks NDErs to explain this sensation in their own words. NDErs were asked, "If your highest level of consciousness and alertness during the experience was different from your normal everyday consciousness and alertness, please explain." Hundreds of NDErs responded to this question, and here are some representative responses.

A woman who was struck by a car wrote,

It was only different in the sense that it was another space and another perception of being. . . . I believe there was an all-around awareness that didn't require thought in the way that our minds—brains, rather—are programmed and designed to register them. This is beyond light speed, if you will.

A man whose pulse and breathing stopped experienced the following:

During the entire incident, I felt as though I had never been more alert. My mind was fast, even though physically I was unconscious.

UNLIKE DREAMS OR DEATH

Responses like these suggest that consciousness continues after death. To understand how remarkable it is to have a conscious experience at the time of clinical death, it is helpful to understand what happens at the moment of death. Many NDEs are associated with a cardiac arrest, which means the heart stops beating.[1] Among those having a cardiac arrest, about 10 to 20 percent will have a near-death experience.[2] At the time of a life-threatening event, it cannot be predicted who will have a near-death experience and who will not.

As discussed in chapter 2, when the heart stops beating, blood immediately stops flowing to the brain. Approximately ten to twenty seconds after blood stops flowing to the brain, the electroencephalogram (EEG), which measures brain electrical activity, goes flat. The EEG measures electrical activity in the cortex, or outer part of the brain, which is responsible for conscious thought. Following cardiac arrest a lucid, organized, and conscious experience should be impossible.

With a flat EEG, it is still possible for electrical activity to be present in the lower parts of the brain, such as the brain stem. There is no chance that electrical activity in these lower parts of the brain could account for such a highly lucid and ordered experience as described by NDErs.

Lucidity coupled with the predictable order of elements establishes that NDEs are not dreams or hallucinations, nor are they due to any other causes of impaired brain functioning.

The first version of the NDERF survey asked, "Was the experience dreamlike in any way?" and allowed only a narrative answer. The response to this question was generally an adamant *no!* This indicates that NDErs were not having dreams. This finding is especially significant given that the wording of the question encouraged a positive response if *any* part of the NDE was dreamlike.

The lucidity of the near-death experience becomes apparent when we look at descriptions of vision during NDEs. In the many hundreds of NDE case studies I have reviewed, descriptions of vision are often so dramatic that I must remind myself that the NDErs are generally unconscious and often clinically dead at the time they are experiencing extraordinary vision. Colors are often described as unworldly in their variety and beauty. Once again, I am showing several random examples from the NDERF case studies to illustrate the lucidity of vision in NDEs.

A man who experienced three near-death experiences wrote,

The colors on the other side are the brightest colors; our most fluorescent colors on this earth are muddy [compared] to the brightness and vividness of the colors that are in Heaven.

A woman who suffered a heart attack and stroke reported,

I wanted to see color again, and when I did it was fantastic! I saw colors I could never explain. A shade of red that I will never forget.

A woman who was unresponsive after a motorcycle accident said,

I was taken to a beautiful meadow with the most gorgeous plant life and colors so vibrant that I've never seen anywhere; it was amazing!

Leading NDE researcher Dr. Greyson is seeing the same lucidity and higher level of consciousness in the NDEs he studies as I am seeing in the NDERF study. Dr. Greyson and his coresearchers say,

Near-death experiencers often describe their mental processes during the NDE as remarkably clear and lucid and their sensory experiences as unusually vivid, surpassing those of their normal waking state. An analysis of 520 cases in our collection showed that 80 percent of experiencers described their thinking during the NDE as "clearer than usual" or "as clear as usual." Furthermore, in our collection, people reported enhanced mental functioning significantly more often when they were actually physiologically close to death than when they were not.[3]

BEYOND NORMAL SENSES

Vision during NDEs is usually different from earthly vision. An NDERF survey question asked, "Did your vision differ in any way from your normal, everyday vision (in any aspect, such as clarity, field of vision, colors, brightness, depth perception, degree of solidness/transparency of objects, etc.)?" Of the 613 NDErs responding, 66.1 percent answered "Yes," 15.0 percent answered "Uncertain," and only 18.9 percent answered "No." Hundreds of NDErs then provided a narrative explanation of how vision during their NDEs differed from earthly vision. Review of these narratives reveals that many NDErs describe vision as unworldly in its brightness, clarity, and vividness. Very few NDErs described their NDE vision as diminished in comparison to their earthly vision.

Many NDErs indicate they have 360-degree vision during their experience, sometimes even more than that. The term *360 degrees* refers to two dimensions only, while NDErs often report spherical, three-dimensional visual awareness simultaneously in all directions—forward, backward, right, left, above, and below.

For example, a child we'll call Ray was horsing around on a school playground. His friend wanted to show him a new judo throw. Ray was thrown and was knocked senseless when he landed on his head. He could see simultaneously in all directions. As he recounted the event,

I still had a "body," but it was entirely different. I could see in three dimensions as if I had no body at all but was just a floating eyeball, for lack of a better explanation. I could see all directions at once, yet there were no directions or dimensions as we think of them.

People who have had near-death experiences often describe enhanced and even supernormal vision. This is powerful evidence that something other than the physical brain is responsible for vision during NDEs. We will explore this concept further in chapter 5 when we examine visual NDEs in the blind, including those blind from birth.

The sense of hearing during a near-death experience may be different from everyday hearing, but to a lesser degree than noted with vision. The NDERF survey asked NDErs, "Did your hearing differ in any way from your normal, everyday hearing (in any aspect, such as clarity, ability to recognize source of sound, pitch, loudness, etc.)?" To this question 46.0 percent of NDErs answered "Yes," 22.2 percent answered "Uncertain," and 31.8 percent answered "No." Many went on to describe what they meant.

One such description came from Mark, a young man who was found to have an obstructed artery in his heart. The cardiologist tried to insert a device called a stent into the artery, but a complication developed requiring emergency surgery. While recovering from surgery, Mark's weakened heart stopped.

As the doctors worked feverishly to bring him back, Mark took a journey down "the most beautiful road I have ever seen," one that took him through a mountain paradise. As he took a walk through this heavenly place, Mark began to hear a voice that seemed to be "from nowhere, yet everywhere."

"Mark! You must go back!"

"Go back? No! No! I can't go back!"

Again the voice said, "You must return; I have given you [a] task; you have not finished."

"No, no, please, God, no! Let me stay."

With lightning speed, I was naked moving backward through the darkest of darkness. There were lightning bolts all about me, from my feet to the top of my head. Enormous lightning bolts! Going in all directions into the darkness. Despite the brightness of the lightning, the light from it did not penetrate the awful darkness.

Mark recovered. Later, when he described his experience for the NDERF website, Mark indicated that of all the sensory events of that day, one that stood out was the unique clarity of the sound. As Mark said:

All sound was incredibly clear. The voice of the Supreme Being seemed to emanate from nowhere but at the same time from everywhere. Words did not come from the mouths of beings, but from the aura around them.

Here are some other descriptions from NDErs that emphasize the quality of sound during their NDEs:

[I heard] sound, and it wasn't like the sound we hear in our ears. It didn't seem to be coming from anywhere; it was just there. It did not seem to be there because of vibration or wind or anything. I can't describe it.

Clearer and crisper, as if in a chamber of silence listening to whispers.

Superclear. I am slightly hard of hearing. During that time I could hear everything. Superhearing would be a better term.

SOUNDS OF SILENCE

Before you assume that NDEs always produce a stereophonic treat, consider this: the NDERF study found that the absence of sound during a near-death experience is more common than prior research has revealed. In our study, many NDErs experienced noticeable silence during their NDE. And that silence seems to be comforting for most who experience it. One eloquent NDEr said,

I left my body to the wonderful sound of silence, pure loving, graceful silence.

Another respondent, Joseph, described an experience that took place during an asthma attack that was so severe his medications had no effect and he began to thrash for breath. As Joseph told it:

I could feel myself thrashing, but it was this other feeling that I was most concerned about. There was this overwhelming feeling of energy coming over my entire body. I tried to fight it off with willpower, but it kept coming stronger and stronger and stronger, and finally I couldn't keep it at bay any longer. I remember thinking to myself, "I just can't do it anymore."

Then as soon as I thought it, pop! This stillness came over me and my thoughts, [and] I wasn't scared anymore. It was insanely quiet, and I realized that I was still there—and standing, no less (which was impossible due to the fact that I [had] just collapsed backward a few minutes earlier)—and then it dawned on me that I had just passed on. Wow!

This profound lack of sound seems to have had a deep effect. Joseph wrote:

There was no sound at all. It was the most peaceful silence I have ever experienced. Kind of like being submerged in water, with no one else around to make a sound. Thick, thick silence.

The experience was not uncomfortable for Joseph; rather, it was like being in a "state of meditation." This intense silence, which Joseph links to a sense of peace, has carried over into his life. Now, says Joseph, he is much calmer and low-key than before his experience:

The things I got aggravated over in the past no longer have the same effect. If I go into my memory, I seem to have the ability to feel it all over again at will.

All five of the human senses of seeing, hearing, touch, taste, and smell have been described in NDEs. Heightened senses, enhanced vision and hearing, and accelerated consciousness are some of the most dramatic aspects of NDEs. Clearly, these enhanced senses are not in keeping with the clinical meaning of *unconscious* or *clinically dead*. It is medically inexplicable for anyone to have a heightened sense of consciousness while being at the brink of death. These experiences are not dreams or illusory fragments of memory from a dying brain. Near-death experiences are real. There are no other experiences of altered consciousness in which the experiences are so lucid, consciousness is so enhanced, and the experiences are so consistently ordered as in NDEs. The NDERF study, and virtually every study published in this field, shows this consistent pattern of heightened senses and consciousness, which leads some to call the experience a "lucid death."[4]

SKEPTICS: NDEᴙs MAY NOT BE NEAR DEATH

Still, there are those in the scientific community who don't believe that a lucid death takes place. Some of them feel that in prior near-death-experience studies the definition of *near death* was too loose and that it included those who are not physically near death. Perhaps, the skeptics speculate, prior NDE studies included many case studies of those who were not truly near death. The lucid experiences would be explained by the fact that these people did not really have a close brush with death.

For the NDERF research we took these concerns into consideration. The NDERF study included only those people who reported an imminent, life-threatening event at the time of their NDE. The NDERF definition of such an event is very strict and includes only events in which people are physically compromised to the extent that death would be imminent without a change in their physical condition. Generally speaking, the individual reports being so physically compromised that they are unconscious and often clinically dead. Anyone who does not fit this definition is not included in our study.

One of the more common skeptical "explanations" of NDE has been hypoxia. *Hypoxia* means reduced oxygen levels in the blood and the tissues of the body, including the brain. Hypoxia may occur in a variety of conditions including cardiac arrest and other life-threatening events that result in loss of consciousness. Most doctors are quite familiar with the symptoms of hypoxia, which may include headaches, confusion, memory loss, and fatigue. As hypoxia worsens, it may result in increasing confusion and finally unconsciousness. If you have ever found yourself extremely short of breath for any reason, you may have experienced some of the symptoms of hypoxia. If so, unless your hypoxia was so severe that it was a life-threatening event, I am sure what you experienced had nothing in common with the elements of a near-death experience. Near-death experiences almost never have confused memories that are typical of the experience of hypoxia. The fact that highly lucid and organized near-death experiences occur at a time of severe hypoxia is further evidence of the extraordinary and inexplicable state of consciousness that typically occurs during NDEs.

RESPONDING TO THE "OPRAH FACTOR"

Another appropriate concern from the skeptics is whether the content of people's reported NDEs is influenced by how much they know about NDEs at the time of their experience. Some of the more clever researchers call this the "Oprah factor" because of the great job Oprah Winfrey's television show has done to increase knowledge of NDEs.

The skeptics' reasoning goes like this: If the NDEr is aware of NDEs at the time of their own experience, will that affect what they share about their own experience later?

Before the 1975 publication of Dr. Raymond Moody's book *Life After Life* there would have been no possibility of this happening because the general public did not yet know the specific elements of the NDE.

Still, as a skeptic in my own right, I conducted a study to see if the Oprah factor had indeed affected what NDErs share. The study was a simple one. I compared responses to twenty-one survey questions in our first NDERF survey from people whose NDEs occurred before 1975 with people whose NDEs occurred after 1975.[5]

To tell you the truth, the results surprised me. The same NDE elements occurred in the pre-1975 group as in the post-1975 group. What is more, the same elements took place with the same frequency. This study strongly suggests that the content of NDEs is not influenced by prior knowledge of NDEs.

Another and even more convincing study was conducted by Geena Athappilly, MD, and associates in 2006. She reviewed twenty-four NDEs that were shared and recorded prior to 1975, before NDE was publicly known, with a matched group of twenty-four accounts shared after 1975. Her study found that the NDEs from these two different time periods differed only in that NDEs recorded after 1975 showed more frequent description of a tunnel. The authors concluded: "These data challenge the hypothesis that near-death experience accounts are substantially influenced by prevailing cultural models."[6]

The Oprah factor was also addressed by the NDERF survey question "Did you have any knowledge of near-death experience (NDE) prior to your experience?" Of all NDErs surveyed, 66.4 percent responded "No," which I felt was a surprisingly high percentage.

STANDARD LOGIC DOES NOT APPLY

I have looked at thousands of case studies filled with solid evidence of a lucid death. The only conclusion I can come to is that consciousness leaves the body at death.

I know this means that standard logic does not apply— that death might not really mean a final death as we have come to know it. That is why this chapter is titled "Lucid Death." I believe that having a vivid and conscious experience at the time of clinical death is among the best evidence available to suggest a conscious existence after bodily death. It presents one of the strongest lines of evidence of the afterlife.

PROOF #2: OUT OF BODY

In order to experience everyday spirituality, we
need to remember that we are spiritual beings
spending some time in a human body.
—Barbara De Angelis

An out-of-body experience (OBE) is the first element in
many near-death experiences. In the way we have defined it
here, *out of body* means "the separation of consciousness
from the physical body." Describing it in such a mild way
seems almost too tame. Those who have OBEs may report
that when they are in a state of unconsciousness and often
have no pulse they are still able to see earthly, everyday
events. People having OBEs may see their own unconscious
body as well as the frantic activity of medical personnel who
are trying to revive them.

Approximately half of all NDEs have an OBE that involves seeing or hearing earthly events. Usually the point of
consciousness rises above the body. If a ceiling is present, con-

sciousness usually does not rise above the ceiling, at least initially, and is commonly described as residing up in a corner of the room. It is uncommon for the point of consciousness to be at the same level as the body, and only rarely does the point of consciousness move to a location below the body.

Out-of-body experiences have been reported to occur spontaneously, when there is no associated life-threatening event. The term *out-of-body experience* as used in this book refers only to OBEs that occur during NDEs.

Here is an example of an OBE from a man who nearly died from a complication after surgery. As his medical team worked frantically to save his life, he watched from above:

Suddenly my consciousness rose above [my bed in] the ICU. I remember having told myself that I had not had an out-of-body experience so this could not be happening. As I rose, I told myself, "Well, here it is."

The suggestion that OBEs exist may be very difficult for some to accept. This is understandable. Consciousness that exists separately from the physical body is an event that few people have experienced. Before accepting OBEs as factual, reasonable people may require extremely strong evidence for its reality. Such evidence is certainly available, as we shall see.

EXTRABODY VISION

The first large study of out-of-body experiences occurring during near-death experiences was published in 1982 by cardiologist Michael Sabom, MD.[1] He was intrigued by anecdotal reports that he had heard from other doctors. He devised a study in which he interviewed thirty-two NDErs who had out-of-body experiences during their NDEs. Most of these NDErs underwent cardiopulmonary resuscitation (CPR) at the time of their brush with death.

As part of this study, Sabom interviewed twenty-five "seasoned cardiac patients" who did not have NDEs during their cardiac crises. These twenty-five patients served as a control group in the study. Both groups were then asked to describe their own resuscitations.

Sabom found that the NDErs with out-of-body experiences were far more precise than those in the control group in accurately describing their resuscitations. In short, the results of this study were consistent with NDErs' claims that they actually did witness their own resuscitation in the out-of-body state.

A study similar to Sabom's was published in 2004 by Penny Sartori, PhD.[2] She interviewed fifteen NDErs and found that eight of them had experienced being out of body. Like Sabom, she asked the OBErs to describe their own resuscitation efforts and compared their responses to a control group in which the patients had undergone resuscitation but did not have an out-of-body experience.

Sartori found that several NDErs in this study provided remarkably accurate accounts in their out-of-body observations. The control group was highly inaccurate. Several NDErs were inaccurate in their observations, though this might be attributable to effects on their memory by medications administered to sedate them following resuscitation. Many in the control group could only guess at what had taken place or describe what they knew of resuscitation from television. This study is further evidence that those who have out-of-body experiences may indeed be witnessing their own resuscitation at a time when they are clinically dead.

Janice Holden, PhD, a professor of counseling at the University of North Texas, conducted another important study of OBEs.[3] Holden compiled all of the out-of-body accounts in all of the scholarly books and articles published about NDEs. Only accounts where the NDErs later sought to verify the accuracy of their OBE observations were included in the Holden study. This ambitious effort yielded eighty-nine case reports involving observations of earthly, everyday events by people who reported being out of body. An additional fourteen case reports involved observations during the NDE of "nonmaterial, nonphysical phenomena" that could be verified by later earthly observations. Four case reports in this study included both types of NDE observations.

Holden was a stickler for accuracy in this study. She considered the OBErs' "earthly observation" to be inaccurate if even one detail of the observations was found to be inaccurate during later investigations. So if NDE observations were fully 99 percent accurate, the 1 percent that was inaccurate would lead the NDE observations overall to be labeled as inaccurate in this study. Even with such strict criteria, the study found that 92 percent of the NDErs had observations of earthly, everyday events that seemed completely accurate, with no error whatsoever as verified by investigations after the NDE.

One of my favorite out-of-body stories comes from an NDE reported by Kimberly Clark Sharp, a noted NDE researcher in Seattle, Washington.[4] In 1984 Sharp reported a case study in which a woman named Maria was rushed to the hospital with a severe heart attack. After successful resuscitation, Maria told Sharp about her near-death experience, including detailed out-of-body observations of her resuscitation. Then she went one step beyond. Her consciousness passed outside the hospital, she said, where she observed a tennis shoe on the third-story window ledge of the hospital. Maria provided detailed information about the shoe. It was a man's shoe, she said, left-footed and dark blue with a wear mark over the little toe and a shoelace tucked under the heel.

Being the dedicated researcher that she is, Sharp went window to window on the hospital's third floor looking on the ledges. Finally she found the shoe, exactly as Maria had described it. This account stands as remarkably evidential in spite of the efforts of some skeptics to cast doubts.[5]

Another widely quoted experience of OBE perception was reported by Pim van Lommel, MD, and published in *The Lancet*, one of the world's most prestigious medical journals.[6] The patient suffered a cardiac arrest and was not breathing. At the time that a tube was being placed in the airway to ventilate him, it was noted he had upper dentures. The dentures were removed and placed in a crash-cart drawer while the patient was deeply comatose. Over a week later the patient reported having an OBE and accurately described the room he was resuscitated in and the people present. Remarkably, he declared that his lost dentures could be found in the crash-cart drawer. Note that the patient reported seeing the nurse and those present during his resuscitation, which doesn't occur unless someone is lucid and in an out-of-body state.

STUDYING HUNDREDS OF OBEs AT NDERF

The NDERF study uncovered hundreds of accounts of NDEs that included out-of-body experiences. I have studied them in a way similar to the previously discussed Holden study, but with some important differences. For the out-of-body experience study, I personally reviewed 617 sequentially shared NDEs that were posted on NDERF. All near-death experiences meeting the study criteria that were shared on the NDERF questionnaire form from October 10, 2004, to October 10, 2008, were reviewed. The study criteria were that the near-death experience accounts be shared by the individual who personally had the NDE, describe a single NDE, and be shared in English, plus we needed to be allowed to post the NDE on the NDERF website. My goal was to see if there were *any* out-of-body observations of earthly events that either the NDErs or I considered to be *not* realistic. If *any* unrealistic out-of-body observations were found, the NDE would be classified as unrealistic.

A questionnaire was prepared for the study of several elements of the near-death experiences, including OBEs. In my review of these 617 near-death experiences, the first question I answered was: "Did they see or hear any earthly events at a time their consciousness seemed separated from their physical body?"

If the answer to that question was "Yes," two additional questions were asked: "Did the [NDEr] later [after the experience] investigate the accuracy of the earthly events they saw or heard during their experience at the time their consciousness seemed separated from their physical body?" The second question asked was: "Is there any reason to doubt . . . that any of the earthly events seen or heard at the time their conscious-ness seemed separated from their physical body were real?"

For each of the preceding survey questions I selected re-sponses that ranged from a definite "Yes" to a definite "No."

The results of the study are astonishing. Of the 617 near-death-experience accounts, 287 (46.5 percent) described OBEs that contained observations of earthly events that would allow others to objectively assess the reality of their observations. Of this group of 287 OBErs, 280 (97.6 percent) were found to have had out-of-body experiences that were *entirely* realistic and lacked *any* content that was unrealistic. Finally, of the 287 OBErs, 65 (23 percent) of the OBErs de-scribed personally investigating the accuracy of their own OBE observations following their NDE. None of these 65 OBErs described any inaccuracy in their OBE observations based on their later investigations.

These are amazing results, given that I would count the out-of-body experience as unrealistic if *any* part of the OBE did not seem real to either me or the NDErs.

Amazing Findings

The finding that nearly all of the hundreds of OBErs' obser-vations of earthly events were realistic provides some of the strongest evidence ever presented that NDEs are real. The best evidence indicates that NDErs really do experience a separation of consciousness from their physical body. It is all the more remarkable that this is occurring at a time when the NDErs are unconscious or clinically dead.

I can't help but marvel at these findings. There is absolutely no scientific or medical explanation for consciousness existing apart from the body. The fact that OBErs report seeing and hearing at a time when their physical eyes and ears are not functioning could have profound implications for scientific thinking about consciousness. The scientific community may now need to wrestle with a profound question: What does it mean to experience sensory perception without the use of the physical senses?

Many hundreds of NDEs that include out-of-body perception have been shared and posted on the NDERF website. Here are some more examples:

Thaddeus, a physician, had a blood infection that was threatening his life. As he lay in an isolation room at the hospital, suddenly his perspective changed:

Lying on my back. Awake. Suddenly I am looking down at myself from the ceiling. My position is reversed; that is, my head is opposite to my feet on the bed. I see myself very clearly. I have normal vision. I am presented with making a decision. No voice. Just "knowledge" that I have a choice. The choice is stay or go. There is absolutely no value to either choice, which surprises me. . . . A sense of absolute calm. I choose "stay." Immediately I am back in my body.

In the summer of 1971 Diane was with her husband in northern Georgia. They were rafting the Chattahoochee River. She was with eight people in a large raft when it flipped and she was held beneath the rapids by the churning action of the water. Stuck beneath the mighty force of the river, Diane ran out of air, blacked out, and then had this remarkable experience:

The next thing I knew I was a hundred feet above the river, looking down at the raft stuck against the rocks below. I saw the two men in the raft looking for me to come out from underneath. I saw the other woman, who had been in our raft, downstream, clinging to a rock. I watched my husband and my teenage sister, who had rafted without incident down the rapids ahead of us, come running back up the hill to find out why all the debris was floating down the river. We had taken everything out of their raft and put it into ours in case they flipped over, but they went down so easily, we just jumped in to follow them down. From above, I watched my husband climb onto a rock in the river. He couldn't hear what the two men still in the raft were shouting to him over the roar of the water. He had no idea where I was or what had happened, but he knew I was missing. He looked as if he wanted to jump in to try to find me, and I suddenly found myself at his side, trying to stop him because he wasn't much of a swimmer and I knew there was no point. When I reached out to stop him, my hand went right through him. I looked at my hand and thought, oh, my god, I'm dead!

. . . The Being of Light told me it was my choice to stay or go but that there was more for me to do in that life and it wasn't quite time for me to leave. Still hesitating, I was told that if I chose to go back, I would be given certain knowledge to take back with me to share with others. After much discussion, I agreed to go back and suddenly found myself in front of a tall, cone-shaped building—so tall it seemed to go on forever. I was told this was the Hall of Knowledge. I entered the building and flew, spiraling upward, through what appeared to be shelves of books, like in a library, many millions of books, and I flew through them all. When I reached the top, I burst through it into a kaleidoscope of colors and, at the same time, my head popped

out of the water. I was downriver about ten yards from the raft.

I immediately became aware of where I was and grabbed for the nearest rock. I was able to pull myself up, and I coughed up a lot of water. I was in a state of shock but needed no medical attention. I don't know how long I was under the raft; no one was looking at their watch at the time. It could have been three or four minutes; it could have been ten. There was no time where I had been.

FUTURE STUDY

At this time there is a major ongoing study directed by Sam Parnia, MD, principal investigator of the AWARE (AWAreness during REsuscitation) study.[7] AWARE involves the collaboration of many major medical centers around the world, and researchers hope to examine some fifteen hundred survivors of cardiac arrest. As the project name implies, researchers will examine the awareness of patients at the time they are experiencing a cardiac arrest. Pictures will be placed in hospital rooms in such a way that they are visible only from the ceiling to determine if they can be seen during the OBE. It will be several years before we have results from this study. Hopefully, this study will answer many further questions about OBEs during NDEs.

There have been several prior studies where targets were placed in areas of hospitals where critically ill patients might have NDEs. These targets were paper or computer screens with visual pictures or words. Targets were usually placed in a location where the patient, and those caring for the patient, would not ordinarily see them. Designers of these studies hoped that patients having an out-of-body experience during an NDE would be able to see the targets and thus provide objective proof of the OBE. So far there have been few NDEs and even fewer OBEs in these studies. None of the OBEs in these studies ever included visual perception directed toward the target.

Personally, I think it is extremely important to continue with this type of research. Not only does it contribute to an understanding of our physical and mental processes, it may also contribute to our understanding of the spiritual world. I am convinced that studying out-of-body experiences in a variety of ways will lead to a clearer understanding of the special state of consciousness consistently described in NDEs.

WHAT THE SKEPTICS SAY

Some skeptics think that out-of-body experiences are simply fragments of memory that pop up as a person begins to die. They suggest that these fragments of memory might arise from what the near-death experiencer was able to hear or feel during the time of apparent unconsciousness. This argument also suggests that out-of-body experiences may be unreal reconstructions of partial memories from the time the NDEr is losing consciousness before the NDE or recovering consciousness immediately after the NDE. That some corroboration of the OBE observations with actual events or objects is found, they say, could be just lucky guesses.

The NDERF study shows that this argument is wrong.

A review of 287 OBE accounts reveals that they are fully realistic, without *any* apparent error, in 97.6 percent of the cases. If OBEs were unreal fragments of memory or lucky guesses, it is unbelievable that there would be such a high percentage of completely accurate OBE observations in hundreds of NDEs.

Research says that memories formed just before or after a period of cardiac arrest, if they occur at all, are marked by confusion.[8] By contrast, NDEs contain confused memories only rarely. If *any* part of the NDE were due to simple reconstruction of memory fragments, such memories would be expected to become progressively more or less confused as the NDEr approached or recovered from unconsciousness. This is not what happens. Near-death experiences are typically highly lucid from beginning to end.

In the NDERF study we ask, "At what time during the experience were you at your highest level of consciousness and alertness?" People are invited to respond with a narrative answer. In reviewing hundreds of responses to this question, we have found that the highest level of consciousness and alertness is usually experienced not at the beginning or end of the NDE but somewhere during or throughout the entire NDE. Very few NDErs describe their highest level of alertness as occurring when they approached or recovered from their time of unconsciousness. This is further strong evidence that the OBEs that take place during near-death experiences are real events, not just memory fragments. In addition, NDERF research shows people in an out-of-body state usually experience a higher level of consciousness and alertness than they experience on a day-to-day basis during their everyday life.

FAR FROM THEIR BODY

There is additional striking evidence that OBEs occurring during near-death experiences are real. This evidence comes from the case studies of those NDErs who say they have left their body and traveled some distance from it, beyond the range of their physical senses. For instance, a patient whose body is being resuscitated in the emergency room might find himself or herself floating out of the room and into another part of the hospital. Later, the person is able to recount accurate observations about what was taking place far from the physical body. Many case reports describing this have been published over the years by NDE researchers.[9] In the previously presented NDERF study of OBE, there were ten OBE observations of earthly events that were clearly far from the physical body and beyond any possible bodily sensory awareness. All ten of these OBE observations were entirely realistic.

Out-of-body experiences containing observations far removed from the body are as realistic as the more common OBEs involving observations of events happening close to the physical body. This example comes from a doctor in India. He made an electrical calling device, but it malfunctioned and he was electrocuted. He was able to see through the walls of his house and saw his father approaching his body. He was able to see details on the roof tiles far above his body:

I rose to about ten feet off the ground, and I stopped, hovering near the roof tiles. I could see the letters written on the roof tiles from very near, almost a few inches. Each letter appeared very big to me.

As a physician, I am startled by such experiences. Even now, after encountering hundreds of out-of-body accounts, I am still sometimes amazed to think that our consciousness may know no bounds.

TRY THIS AT HOME

Still, there may be some who are not yet convinced that OBEs are an authentic phenomenon. Are you still a doubter? Try this experiment: Close your eyes for five minutes in a public place, staying as aware as possible of ongoing events during this time. Have another person there with you who is seeing and hearing events. At the end of five minutes, compare your impressions of the five minutes with the person accompanying you. Even though you were fully alert and trying to be aware of ongoing events, I can guess that your impressions will contain significant inaccuracies—far more than those found in the out-of-body experiences of the subjects in the NDERF study.

PROOF #3: BLIND SIGHT

Seeing is believing, but also know that believing is seeing.
—Dennis Waitley

In 1998 Kenneth Ring, PhD, and Sharon Cooper, MA, published a landmark article in the *Journal of Near-Death Studies* about blind people who have vividly visual near-death experiences or out-of-body experiences not associated with NDEs.[1] An especially interesting subgroup in this study was made up of case reports from individuals who were born totally blind and had NDEs with the typical elements, including detailed visual content. It is medically inexplicable that a person blind either at birth or shortly after birth would have an organized visual NDE.

One such example is the story of Vicki, who saw for the first time in her life during her near-death experience, as documented in Ring and Cooper's book, *Mindsight*. She was blind from shortly after birth because of damage to her optic nerves as a result of receiving too much oxygen in an incubator. Vicki had two near-death experiences. One was at age twelve due to complications of appendicitis, and the second was at age twenty-two following a serious car accident. The first time in her life that she was able to see was during her first near-death experience when she had an OBE. According to Vicki, the content of both near-death experiences was similar, but the NDE following the car accident was more vivid and detailed. Thus, I will present details of her second near-death experience, which occurred after she sustained trauma, including head injuries, so severe that she was still recovering from the accident a year later. As her near-death experience began, she was in "stunned awe" above her body in the emergency room, watching the medical personnel trying to save her. After she calmed down, she had a very detailed and highly visual NDE that included visiting a beautiful unearthly realm, encountering deceased friends, and a life review. She reported her reaction to seeing herself:

> I knew it was me. . . . I was pretty thin then. I was quite tall and thin at that point. And I recognized at first that it was a body, but I didn't even know that it was mine initially. Then I perceived that I was up on the ceiling, and I thought, "Well, that's kind of weird. What am I doing up here?" I thought, "Well, this must be me. Am I dead?" . . . I just briefly saw this body, and . . . I knew that it was mine because I wasn't in mine.[2]

Vicki was married and wearing rings, but of course had never seen them. Here are her recollections of her rings:

I think I was wearing the plain gold band on my right ring finger and my father's wedding ring next to it. But my wedding ring I definitely saw. . . . That was the one I noticed the most because it's unusual. It has orange blossoms on the corners of it.[3]

What is so remarkable about Vicki's recollection of these visual impressions is that she had never before understood the concept of vision. "This was," she said, "the only time I could ever relate to seeing and to what light was, because I experienced it."[4]

MIRACLE VISION

I have interviewed Vicki myself, and I find her story to be remarkable. For those born blind, sight is an abstract concept. They understand the world only from their senses of hearing, touch, taste, and smell. Occasionally, blind people with certain correctable conditions are able to regain their vision through surgical procedures. When blind people acquire sight, there is often a prolonged period of time in which they have trouble making sense of visual perceptions. This contrasts with Vicki, who was immediately aware of her visual perceptions during her NDE. This further suggests that Vicki's vision was not of physical origin.

Studies have shown that the dreams of those born blind do not include vision. Vision cannot be effectively explained to those born blind, even by drawing analogies to the four remaining senses they possess. I tried this in conversations with Vicki and was unsuccessful.

Being blind from birth and suddenly being able to see at the point of death must be both beautiful and frustrating at the same time. A number of the subjects in Ring and Cooper's study tried to explain exactly what they had experienced. Some backed away from saying the experience was visual because they truly didn't know what a visual experience was. After thinking about it, one man declared that his experience was a form of synthesis, which in this case meant a combination of all of his senses to form a new experience. Here is how the subject described it in Ring and Cooper's book, *Mindsight*:

> I think what it was that was happening here was a bunch of synesthesia, where all these perceptions were being blended into some image in my mind, you know, the visual, the tactile, all the input that I had. I can't literally say I really saw anything, but yet I was aware of what was going on, and perceiving all that in my mind. . . . But I don't remember detail. That's why I say I'm loath to describe it as a visual.[5]

Another of Ring's subjects went on to say that his visual NDE went *beyond* the visual:

> What I'm saying is I was more aware. I don't know if it's through sight that I was aware. . . . I'm not sure. All I know is . . . somehow I was aware of information or things that were going on that I wouldn't normally be able to pick up through seeing. . . . That's why I'm being very careful how I'm wording it, 'cause I'm not sure

where it came from. I would say to you I have a feeling it didn't come from seeing, and yet I'm not sure.[6]

After considering the stories told to him by these blind subjects, Ring and Cooper came to a conclusion that seemed to take all sides of the argument into consideration:

Even if we cannot assert that the blind see in these experiences in any straightforward way, we still have to reckon with the fact—and it does seem to be a fact—that they nevertheless do have access to a kind of expanded super-sensory awareness that may in itself not be explicable by normal means. . . . Perhaps, as we have suggested, even if these reports may not in the end represent an analogue of retinal vision as such, they clearly represent something that must be directly addressed. . . .

Indeed, what we appear to have here is a distinctive state of consciousness, which we would like to call transcendental awareness, or mindsight.[7]

I agree with Ring and Cooper. Visual NDEs that happen to the blind appear to involve an unearthly form of visual experience. There is no medical explanation for anyone born blind to have such a visual NDE. Yet blind people who have near-death experiences may immediately have full and clear vision. This is further evidence that vision in NDEs, including near-death experiences in those who are not blind, is unlike ordinary, physical vision.

NDERF has received several near-death accounts from individuals with significant visual impairment or even legal blindness. An example of a near-death experience occurring in an individual with legal blindness comes from Violet. She was having severe bleeding during childbirth, and the doctor thought they had lost her. Violet had an out-of-body experience, and her vision was remarkably clear:

Everything was very bright and sharp. I am legally blind without my glasses, but the nurse took my glasses before they took me to the delivery room, but I could see clearly what the doctor was doing.

BETTER VISION NEAR DEATH

By studying such a huge volume of near-death experiences, we have received a constant stream of answers to questions we have about NDEs and the afterlife. But studying NDEs may be mystifying as well. For every answer we receive, sometimes several other questions present themselves. And one of the big questions for me is: Why—how—can a blind person see during a near-death experience? Add to that another question: What does it mean that a blind person can see during an NDE?

Let me start by considering that first question. Describing vision in the blind as "unearthly" is not a complete answer. There is a transcendental aspect to much in NDE research that remains mysterious. Researching NDEs requires different methodology than is used for most other scientific research. Near-death experiences cannot be reproduced in a laboratory. We cannot wire people with sensitive medical equipment and give them near-death experiences. That would be medically unethical. One thing that we can do is collect and study large numbers of NDE case studies and look for evidence regarding the possibility of an after-life. That is what we have done with the NDERF study.

But by doing this, we have encountered many questions for which we don't yet have complete answers. Why the blind can see during an NDE is one of them. Although we don't have a complete answer, we do have enough data that I can offer some speculation.

It is medically inexplicable for someone born blind to have a detailed and organized visual experience. Another piece of evidence comes from nonblind near-death experiencers who frequently describe unearthly visual ability—360-degree vision, for example. People who have near-death experiences are generally unconscious, and their normal physiologic ability to see is not functioning during their NDEs. All this points to the conclusion that vision described during NDEs is different from earthly vision, which is so familiar to us. Vision in the afterlife may be somewhat analogous to earthly vision but very different in that it is more vivid, comprehensive, and nonphysical.

All five senses associated with earthly life (seeing, hearing, touch, taste, and smell) have been reported in the NDERF case studies. It is without question that NDErs often describe increased function in all of these senses at a time when they should have no sensory function at all. Of all these senses, vision is often described as being very different from ordinary, everyday vision.

The NDERF survey asked NDErs, "Did your vision differ in any way from your normal, everyday vision (in any aspect, such as clarity, field of vision, colors, brightness, depth perception, degree of solidness/transparency of objects, etc.)?" Of the respondents, 66.1 percent answered "Yes," 15.0 percent answered "Uncertain," and only 18.9 percent answered "No." Near-death experiencers were encouraged to provide a narrative response to this question. Here are some of their replies:

My vision was greatly increased. I was able to see things as close or as far as I needed. There was no strain involved; it was almost like auto-zooming a camera. If I felt I needed to see something I just looked at it, no thought or strain required.

When I was floating above my body, I could see 360 degrees around me at the same time. But I only seemed to focus on a smaller visible area similar to my normal physical vision.

It was like watching high-definition TV, as compared to normal: all people and things were vivid; there was no darkness or shadows.

Clarity, bright lights. Looking back, I had perfect eyesight (I am terribly nearsighted); everything was solid.

Vision was blurry in sedation; when I was having the heart attack vision became clear, as my thoughts also did.

I was short-[near]sighted, but at that moment my vision was 100 percent, and . . . everything was super clear and crisp and all colors were brilliant.

Having no material body, I was sensing, seeing, feeling, on another plane. It is like trying to explain the colors of the rainbow to a blind person.

Hundreds of such descriptions of vision during NDEs have been collected at NDERF. Descriptions of vision during NDE are often so dramatic that I have to remind myself that the NDErs are generally unconscious and often clinically dead at the time they are experiencing this extraordinary level of vision. Yet over the years, hundreds of NDE accounts have been submitted to NDERF that commonly describe supernormal vision, accelerated consciousness, realistic out-of-body observations, and many other elements that take place while the NDErs are unconscious or clinically dead.

Understanding what happens during near-death experiences, including the vision described, has required me to consider what I would have thought unthinkable early in my medical career: perhaps NDErs are actually describing another real, transcendental realm of existence. Perhaps the rules we all thought we knew about consciousness and sensory perception need to be reconsidered.

SEEING IS BELIEVING

This takes us back to the second question that the research has posed to me, namely: What does it mean that a blind person can see during an NDE?

I had never even thought of this as a question until I took my son Phillip to a meeting in Seattle where a blind woman talked about her NDE. Phillip was nine years old at the time, and I thought he would be bored with the presentation. But his response was quite the contrary. Her presentation held his rapt attention. When the lecture was over, we walked quietly to the car. I could tell something was on Phillip's mind, so I said nothing, inspiring him to fill the dead air.

Finally Phillip spoke. "If blind people can see during a near-death experience, then the experience must not be caused by brain chemistry," he said. "The experience must be real!"

It's thinking like this that puts blind sight high on my list of evidence for the afterlife.

PROOF #4: IMPOSSIBLY CONSCIOUS

Breath is the bridge which connects life to consciousness,
which unites your body to your thoughts.
—Thich Nhat Hanh

Some near-death experiences take place while a patient is
undergoing surgery and has been anesthetized. It may seem
that a discussion of NDEs occurring while under general
anesthesia belongs with the discussion of NDEs and unconsciousness. However, as we will see, there is a great difference between unconsciousness caused by general anesthetic
and that caused by trauma or serious illness.

The proper use of general anesthetic leads to a controlled,
total unconsciousness. The term *general anesthesia,* according to Merriam-Webster, means "anesthesia affecting the
entire body and accompanied by loss of consciousness."
When anesthetic is correctly administered, the anesthesiolo-

gist knows that the patient has no conscious awareness of his or her surroundings. Essentially, the patient is dead to the world. The term *anesthesia* may refer to either local or general anesthesia. The term *anesthesia* in this chapter will refer only to general anesthesia.

According to textbooks on the subject, general anesthesia is intended to bring about five states during surgery:

- Pain relief
- Loss of memory of the procedure, commonly known as amnesia
- Loss of consciousness
- Motionlessness
- Reduced autonomic nerve responses, meaning reduced heart rate, slower breathing, or lower-than-normal blood pressure

In order to properly care for a patient who is undergoing anesthesia, the anesthesiologist connects the patient to a variety of monitors to observe heart and breathing rate and blood gases. Anesthesia involves intensive efforts to make certain that loss of consciousness and a state of amnesia are achieved and maintained. Yet many near-death experiences are reported by patients who almost died while under this carefully monitored blanket of anesthesia.

What life-threatening events can occur under anesthesia? Sometimes these patients are already near death from a life-threatening illness or injury requiring emergency surgery and they suffer a heart attack, or perhaps they are allergic to the medications given. Or the surgery may have complications and the patient is exposed to a near-death situation.

I have been surprised at the large number of patients who can recount vivid NDEs during anesthesia. The high level of awareness expressed in these case studies is further strong evidence of a nonearthly state of consciousness during NDEs that even anesthesia cannot dampen.

FIVE CASE STUDIES: NDEs THAT TOOK PLACE UNDER ANESTHESIA

Jaime was undergoing surgery when the tube that was inserted for his breathing became clogged. The doctors later told him that he had been "code blue" and had to have defibrillator paddles applied to be resuscitated. Here is what happened.

Now, all I remember was being anesthetized. The next thing I [knew], I [was] still on my back. At first it seemed like there was nothingness, like I was on my back afloat, and it was pitch-dark, a very scary darkness. I remember I kept putting my hands in front of my face; I could not see them or my body, but I knew that they were there. Then I start hearing this low hummmm, and it was like being underwater, like when you are under and you can hear noise and it's muffled, that kind of thing. Anyway, I was wondering why it was so dark. Nothing else mattered. I could not remember anything prior to this—not the surgery, anything. It was like this was the only thing I could think of.

I then noticed that while it was pitch-dark, it felt as if I was in a tunnel, and all along the tunnel were doorways, but the whole tunnel I could sense was like . . . a cave—sort of rocky, not too rocky but kind of smooth—at least that's my impression of it.

So then I am feeling a little more afraid, like, what's going on here? It felt like I was like that for an hour. Just there, then, I could see a pinpoint of white light in front of me in the distance, the size of a pencil eraser head—that size. So I sense that I start moving in that direction, . . . like something [is] pulling me there; I don't feel as if I [am] doing it. At this point I was like floating [in an] upright position, then going slowly toward that pinpoint of light. And then I knew that there [were] little doorways all along this tunnel, and I felt that . . . if I wanted to, [I could] go into any of those doorways, and I felt at the time that if I did, I would not come back, but my attention was on the light.

In an instant, I thought, "Grandma," and I was instantly in the light. I kept saying, "You're not dead. I am not dead, you're not dead." She said, "No, I am not, and you are not either." My grandmother had died three years prior, but at that moment I could not remember that, just that she was not dead and that she was so alive and well. She had died of dementia complications. She invited me to sit and have coffee like we used to all the time at her house. Her table was there, the chairs. She looked like she did when she was in her thirties. She had on a purple dress, like a nice one she had with flowers on it, except that the flowers seemed to glow a fluorescent yellow.

Then I noticed that there was a fluorescent light that emanated from the top of the room, and I started feeling so good-like. I can't describe it—love, or like the first time you kiss. Electricity. Butterflies in your stomach, like the best drug. I don't know how to describe it, it felt so good.

I then kind of got a little panicky 'cause I noticed that there was no light source; it was just there. That's when she touched my hand, [and] I noticed that I looked down and could see my hand also. It was there, but it looked white, almost fluorescent, and she told me that it was all right. (All this conversation was in Spanish, by the way.) And she said, let's drink the coffee. I did. But I notice[d] that it was not hot and had no taste. It was luke-warm, but yet there was steam coming from it, like it was hot but was not. It's like when you are sick and there's no taste.

Anyway, I tell her that we [the family] think of her every day. She stated that she knew. She knew that we loved her very much and she loved us.

And then I noticed that the room was domelike, that in one section, the left side of that domed room, was like a curtain, and I saw my grandfather on my mom's side peek through, and I [saw] another lady, heavyset, short, with a long black pony-tail. I wanted to say something, and that is when my grand-mother told me, "You have to go; you can't stay here; it's not your time."

I then felt terrible; I started to cry. I told her, "But, Grandma, I want to stay here." It felt so wonderful I did not want to leave. I remember begging in Spanish, "Please, I want to stay with you. I never want to leave here."

She said, "You will be back here when it's your time; don't worry." Then she said, "Tell everyone I love them and think of them all the time."

At this point I was still saying, "But, but I wanna stay," and then I heard this loud pop. It felt like I was hit in the chest with a sledgehammer made of fire. I remember coming to and gagging. I was on life support—all the tubes, etc. I felt terrible. I noticed *my dad was there and the rest of the family. I don't remember what happened next, but I do remember telling him that I needed a paper. I had to write something: "I seen Grandma."*

Cyndi was having a second heart valve replacement surgery within six months when she had the experience she described below. She asked her doctor if it was possible to dream during surgery. When he said no, she replied, "Then we have to talk." Here is a paraphrase of what she experienced.

During my surgery I felt myself lift from my body and go above the operating table. The doctor told me later that they had kept my heart open and stopped for a long time, and they had a great amount of difficulty getting my heart started again. That must have been when I left my body because I could see the doctors nervously trying to get my heart going. It was strange to be so detached from my physical body. I was curious about what they were doing but not concerned. Then, as I drifted farther away, I saw my father at the head of the table. He looked up at me, which did give me a surprise because he had been dead now for almost a year.

Valerie was seventeen years old and undergoing surgery. During the operation her heart stopped. Here is her experience:

Sometime during surgery I went through a tunnel. Parts of my life passed me by. I had closed my eyes tight; I remember someone saying, open your eyes. I was in a pure white space and could see rooms with spirits walking around. I started to cry, but no tears. I remember looking at my hands, and they were translucent. Then an angel appeared; she had such a radiant glow to her beauty to behold. She comforted me, telling me I was safe. I remember telling her I wasn't ready to die. She said she knew that. Then she pointed down, and I could see the doctors doing CPR on a little girl. Not really understanding that was me, I watched my whole operation, CPR and all. I told her that was so sad, she looks so young. Then she said they are bringing her back, and I felt like I was pushed and thrown back into that painful body.

Patricia was scheduled for a two-hour surgery to remove her gallbladder. The surgery lasted eight hours, and her heart stopped twice:

The next thing I knew, I heard the doctor yelling and the nurses running around. I looked to my right and saw the doctor beating on my chest, but all I could do was stand there until I saw a light on the wall. It looked like a flashlight that grew bigger, and I touched it and was taken into a tunnel with clouds spinning and rolling around. The clouds were gray, white, and smoky somewhat. I was gliding very fast with my arms just dangling. When I got to the end the light turned orange and there [was a] very tall man dressed in [a] tan work outfit (shirt & pants). I look[ed] pas[t] him, and I could see yellow flowers and a large mountain and a blue sky. His face was the color of light sand, and his hair was golden tan. He had the kindest look in his eyes. I could hear the silence and see the trees, and I wanted to run in, but he stopped me. He tilted me backwards and sent me back through the tunnel with a gentle push, at which time I heard the doctor say, we got her. There was no pain when I was back in my body, only a fullness of some sort around my chest and stomach.

Christopher was being treated surgically for a serious heart disease. He was under partial anesthesia, called "conscious sedation." He was heavily sedated and had a heart attack. Christopher describes how he became *more* conscious after his heart attack, a seemingly impossible occurrence:

I recently found out that I have Wolff-Parkinson-White Syndrome/heart disease, which causes sudden death at any moment because of the extra [electrical] pathway in the heart. The only way to fix this heart disease is by ablation, which is surgery where the surgeon removes the extra [electrical] pathway in the heart. I was under a conscious sedation. I felt sedated to the point where I did not know what was happening to me, but there was a moment when I went into V tach [ventricular tachycardia], where the heart speeds up so fast it causes a heart attack. Even under the sedation I felt a small amount of pain, but when my heart started going into V tach, a peace came over me. I became fully aware of my surroundings. I could feel the shell of my body, and my spirit began to rise; an extreme peace came over me. As my spirit began to rise, the doctor shocked me and then again, and my spirit stopped and went back into my body, and [my] state of mind went back to being sedated. I felt complete peace, no worries about anything, and it was one of the greatest experiences of my life.

LUCID YET UNCONSCIOUS

In prior chapters I presented the responses to survey questions from the NDERF study of 613 NDErs, all with NDE Scale scores of 7 and higher. To compare the content of NDEs occurring under general anesthesia to all other NDEs, I used this same group of 613 NDErs.

This study included twenty-three NDErs who described their experiences as having occurred while under general anesthesia. Many of these accounts described a cardiac arrest as the associated life-threatening event while under general anesthesia.

These NDEs occurring under general anesthesia were compared to the remaining 590 NDEs in the NDERF study by reviewing the responses of both groups to thirty-three survey questions that asked about NDE content. We compared the responses to these thirty-three questions between the two groups using a statistical tool called chi-square. Due to the large number of questions asked about the content of the NDE, the responses between the two groups were considered different only if there was a statistically determined less than 1 in 100 chance that the differences in responses could be due to chance. A *trend* toward a statistically significant difference was defined as a 3 in 100 chance that the differences in responses between the two groups could be due to chance.

The results: there were no significant differences in the responses to any of the thirty-three survey questions between the two groups, with the exception that anesthesia-associated NDEs reported encountering a tunnel more often. Near-death experiences described as occurring under general anesthesia had all the NDE elements as those not occurring under general anesthesia. Remarkably, NDE elements appear to occur with the same frequency, with the exception of a tunnel experience, regardless of whether or not the NDEr was under general anesthesia at the time of their experience.

If consciousness were only a product of the physical brain, then it would make sense that NDEs under general anesthesia would have less consciousness and alertness during their experiences than other NDEs, right? This is certainly what would be expected, but it is not what the NDERF study found. An NDERF survey question asks, "How did your highest level of consciousness and alertness during the experience compare to your normal everyday consciousness and alertness?" For the NDEs described as occurring under general anesthesia, 83 percent of the respondents answered "More consciousness and alertness than normal" to this question, compared to 74 percent for all other NDEs. The responses to this question by the two groups were not statistically significantly different.

These are incredible results! Either general anesthesia alone *or* cardiac arrest alone produces unconsciousness with no possibility of a lucid memory. Recall our prior discussion that ten to twenty seconds after a cardiac arrest the EEG, a measure of brain electrical activity, goes flat, indicating no measurable electrical brain activity. The occurrence of typical NDEs under general anesthesia is thus doubly medically inexplicable. The finding that typical NDEs occur while under general anesthesia is among the strongest evidence yet presented that consciousness can exist apart from the body.

Other NDE researchers have reported NDEs that take place while under general anesthesia. Bruce Greyson, MD, at the University of Virginia, states, "In our collection of NDEs, 127 out of 578 NDE cases (22 percent) occurred under general anesthesia, and they included such features as OBEs that involved experiencers' watching medical personnel working on their bodies, an unusually bright or vivid light, meeting deceased persons, and thoughts, memories, and sensations that were clearer than usual."[1]

MATERIAL BEINGS WITH SOULS

Sir John Eccles was a Nobel Prize–winning neuroscientist who studied consciousness. He proposed that consciousness may actually exist apart from the brain. Eccles once stated, "I maintain that the human mystery is incredibly demeaned by scientific reductionism, with its claim in promissory materialism to account eventually for all of the spiritual world in terms of patterns of neuronal activity. This belief must be classed as a superstition. . . . We have to recognize that we are spiritual beings with souls existing in a spiritual world as well as material beings with bodies and brains existing in a material world."[2]

SKEPTICS: TOO LITTLE ANESTHESIA

There are skeptics, of course. And the ones speaking out on this subject say that experiences like these can only be the result of too little anesthesia being used, leading to partial consciousness during the operation.

To say this, of course, is to ignore NDEs resulting from anesthetic overdose. And it also ignores the type of experiences reported by patients who do actually awaken from anesthesia during surgery. Fortunately, only 1 to 3 in 1,000 patients[3] experience this "anesthetic awareness."

Rather than the type of coherent NDEs you read here, anesthetic awareness results in totally different experiences.[4] Those who experience anesthetic awareness often report very unpleasant, painful, and frightening experiences. Unlike NDEs, which are predominantly visual experiences, this partial awakening during anesthesia more often involves brief and fragmented experiences that may involve hearing, but usually not vision. I would emphasize that partial awakening during anesthesia is very rare and should not be a serious cause of worry about an anesthetic procedure.

When near-death experiences occur during general anesthesia, there are often OBE observations of the operation. During these out-of-body experience observations, NDErs typically see their own resuscitation taking place on the operating table. These near-death experiencers are not seeing themselves with too little anesthesia; they are seeing themselves coding. What the near-death experiencers see confirms that their NDEs are occurring at the time of a life-threatening event, usually a cardiac arrest.

Near-death experiences that occur during cardiac arrest while under general anesthesia are perhaps the strictest test of the possibility of consciousness residing outside of the body. By conventional medical thinking, neither a person under anesthesia nor a person experiencing cardiac arrest should have a conscious experience like that of an NDE. Yet the NDERF study found many that do.

Over twenty different "explanations" of near-death experience have been suggested by skeptics over the years. If there were one or even several "explanations" of NDE that were widely accepted as plausible by the skeptics, there would not be so many different "explanations." The existence of so many "explanations" suggests that there are not any "explanations" of NDE that the skeptics agree on as plausible.

A study by Kevin Nelson, MD, and colleagues suggested a connection between REM intrusion and NDEs.[5] REM is an abbreviation for rapid eye movement. REM commonly occurs as a normal part of sleep, often in association with muscle paralysis. REM sleep commonly includes bizarre and frightening dream imagery. If REM occurs during a time of partial or complete wakefulness, the imagery of these dreams intruding into wakefulness is called REM intrusion. I coauthored a response to Dr. Nelson's paper in which we pointed out that REM intrusion and NDEs are very different experiences. In addition, REM intrusion cannot explain near-death-experience content under circumstances where REM intrusion should not be possible, including NDEs in those blind from birth and NDEs during general anesthesia.[6]

Neuroscientists like Eccles have suggested that consciousness may separate from our material body. It caused him to ponder not only the meaning of life, but also exactly what we mean by the concept of death. We know what happens to the corporeal body when it expires, but what about the soul? It was a question he was never able to answer to his full satisfaction, but he nonetheless commented on it: "We can regard the death of the body and brain as dissolution of our dualist existence," said the Nobel Prize winner. "Hopefully, the liberated soul will find another future of even deeper meaning and more entrancing experiences, perhaps in some renewed embodied existence."[7]

There is no explanation for NDEs occurring under anesthesia other than accepting that full consciousness can exist apart from the physical body. For that reason, I consider them significant evidence of the afterlife.

PROOF #5: PERFECT PLAYBACK

Life is as tedious as a twice-told tale.
—**William Shakespeare**

We will next explore an especially interesting element of near-death experience: the *life review*. What exactly is a life review? There is no better way to answer that question than to actually read one from the NDERF study.

This is a life review from a young man named Mark. He was a passenger in a Jeep that lost control on a snowy road near Lake Tahoe and slammed into a telephone pole. Mark was seriously injured as he was crushed between the Jeep and telephone pole. As a result of this traumatic accident, he had a full-blown near-death experience, one that contained most of the elements outlined in the beginning of this book. One of those elements was a profound life review.

Before you read this, note that there are certain elements common to profound life reviews. For example, Mark sees real events from his life as though they are scenes from a movie about himself. Many near-death experiencers describe their life reviews using terms like *movie*, and they are not bizarre dream images. He also has an empathic reaction to what he is reexperiencing. In essence, he is able to feel how he has made others feel during certain events in his life. He also comes to several conclusions about his life and about life itself.

The self-knowledge that Mark gained through his NDE helped give him direction so that he made important changes in the rest of his life. Mark now thinks about death differently. As he wrote on his NDERF survey form: "All life ends in death. . . . It is not to be feared. . . . Was it Peter Pan who said, 'To die is the greatest adventure'? You will all take this trip. At the moment of death let go of the fear and enjoy the ride."

Here is Mark's life review:

It is unclear how we started, only that the result of this first message was for me to begin a series of feelings about my life. It was the proverbial "life flashing before my eyes" or life review, as I have since heard it called. I would describe this as a long series of feelings based on numerous actions in my life. The difference was that not only did I experience the feelings again, but I had some sort of empathetic sense of the feelings of those around me who were affected by my actions. In other words, I also felt what others felt about my life. The most overwhelming of these feelings came from my mother.

I was adopted as an infant. I had been somewhat of a trou-

blemaker. I sometimes hurt other children when smaller and had taken to drug and alcohol abuse, stealing, crazy driving, bad grades, vandalism, cruelty to my sister, cruelty to animals—the list goes on and on. All of these actions were relived in a nutshell, with the associated feelings of both myself and the parties involved. But the most profound was a strange sense coming from my mother. I could feel how she felt to hear of my death. She was heartbroken and in great pain, but it was all mixed up with feelings of how much trouble I had been in. I got a sense that it was such a tragedy to have had this life end so soon, having never really done much good.

This feeling left me with a sense of having unfinished business in life. The grief that I felt from my mother and friends was intense. In spite of my troubled life, I had many friends, some of whom were close. I was well known if not popular, and I could sense many things said about my life and death. The sense of my mother's grief was overwhelming.

CHANCE TO CHANGE

Life reviews like Mark's are among the most transformative and powerful aspects of the near-death experience. Because of its very nature—sometimes a three-dimensional, panoramic review of *everything* significant in the NDEr's life—the life review is considered a condensed form of healing psychotherapy. "One-minute psychotherapy," as Dr. Raymond Moody has called it.[1]

At the very least, life reviews contain fragments of the NDEr's earthly life. Generally speaking, NDErs who have life reviews view themselves from a third-person perspective. They watch themselves interacting with the people in their lives. They see how they treated others and often step into the other person's place so they know how that person felt when interacting with them. As you can imagine, this can be pleasant or unpleasant depending upon the level of kindness involved. A kind act would result in the NDEr feeling the kindness doled out to the other person, while an unkind act would result in feeling the unkindness.

A spiritual being sometimes accompanies the person who is having the life review. This being may serve as a kind of loving guide, assessing the life review from a higher spiritual plane as the NDEr watches, discussing the spiritual ramifications of the events of the NDEr's life. The being's comments may help the NDEr put his or her life into perspective. Near-death experiencers almost never describe feeling negatively judged by this spiritual being, no matter how unkind they were up to that point in their lives. Near-death experiencers who reviewed many of their own prior cruel actions often express great relief that they were not negatively judged during their NDEs.

When playwright George Kaufman said, "You can't take it with you," he was obviously referring to material things. Many near-death-experience researchers have noted that one of the life review's main lessons is that knowledge and love are two elements that we take with us when we die. As a result, life reviews are often one of the most transformative elements of the NDE. Those who have powerful life reviews tend to revere both knowledge and love after their NDE.

Many NDErs say that the life review, of all the elements of the NDE, was by far the greatest catalyst for change. A life review allows NDErs to relive their own lives, mistakes and all. It also gives them a chance to evaluate themselves on their life performance. Many things that seemed insignificant at the time—a small kindness, for instance—turn out to be significant in their own or another person's life. People realize they became angry over things that were not important or that they placed too much significance on unimportant things.

Here are two more examples of life reviews from NDERF:

Roger was returning from Quebec City with a friend when they lost control of the car they were driving and slammed head-on into another vehicle. Roger immediately left his body and saw from above the events that were swirling around the accident scene. Then, said Roger,

I went into a dark place with nothing around me, but I wasn't scared. It was really peaceful there. I then began to see my whole life unfolding before me like a film projected on a screen, from babyhood to adult life. It was so real! I was looking at myself, but better than a 3-D movie as I was also capable of sensing the feelings of the persons I had interacted with through the years. I could feel the good and bad emotions I made them go through. I was also capable of seeing that the better I made them feel, and the better the emotions they had because of me, [the more] credit (karma) [I would accumulate] and that the bad [emotions] would take some of it back . . . just like in a bank account, but here it was like a karma account to my knowledge.

Linda made a medication mistake. Thinking she was supposed to take eight tablets at once rather than eight over the course of a day, as prescribed by her doctor, Linda passed out on her bed and then passed over.

What I find interesting about this NDE resulting from an accidental overdose is the strong elements of empathy it contains. As you can see, Linda's life review is filled with a message of karma:

I saw everything from birth till then in fast motion. Also, while this was happening I could feel the feelings of these events. I could also feel any pain I gave out to others. I also felt the goodness I'd given out. God asked if I was happy with how things went, and I said yes. He asked me how I felt, and I said I was a little nervous. He explained that this was because all my life I felt this way and it is sort of why I didn't handle [life] properly. I was also told that if the bad outweighed the good you [are] left with the bad. So if you were a truly awful person, you'd be feeling quite awful for your time there. Alternately, if you have given out love and goodness and been kind and caring, you'd be up there feeling sheer bliss and good. I was feeling no extreme sense of badness, for lack of a better word. I was feeling happy, light, carefree but a little nervous inside, like I'd been over a hill too fast or ridden a roller-coaster. But all in all, the balance seemed fair and just enough for what I had just been shown. Mostly good stuff had outweighed the bad.

IMPORTANCE OF REVIEW

A study of life reviews was one of the earliest NDERF research projects.[2] This study was conducted by Jody Long, who serves as the NDERF webmaster. She confirmed the importance of the life review in the NDEr's life by reviewing 319 NDEs from people who submitted NDERF case studies. Jody reviewed their narrative responses from the original NDERF survey's question about the life review: "Did you experience a review of past events in your life?"

The answers to these life review questions were studied. Here they are, along with the results:

- *How life review happened:* Almost 26 percent described how the life review occurred. Many described it as like a rerun of a play or film or like watching it on a screen.
- *Content of life review:* More than 21 percent commented on the content of the life review. Near-death experiencers generally noted that they were the ones who judged themselves. During the process they saw the good and bad, the cause and effect of their choices. Many reported that they had a review of feelings rather than a review of visual events. Some say that their review consisted of feeling others' reactions to their earthly actions.

The life review helps the NDEr understand his or her purpose in life. And it is this understanding about who they are that helps them make significant life changes. Here are a few examples of what NDErs experienced during their life reviews.

While in the light I had a life review and saw everything I . . . ever did in my life; every thought, word, deed, action, inaction was shown to me.

The review was very fast, but I seemed to comprehend everything easily despite the speed.

At that moment, I'm not sure exactly when, someone or something began giving me an examination of conscience, and in the blink of an eye images from my life began passing before me, beginning with my childhood. Each image had its counterpart, or as if the actions of my life were being put into a balance.

Everything I ever thought, did, said, hated, helped, did not help, should have helped was shown in front of me, the crowd of hundreds, and everyone like [in] a movie. How mean I'd been to people, how I could have helped them, how mean I was (unintentionally also) to animals! Yes! Even the animals had had feelings. It was horrible. I fell on my face in shame. I saw how my acting, or not acting, rippled in effect towards other people and their lives. It wasn't until then that I understood how each little decision or choice affects the world. The sense of letting my Savior down was too real. Strangely, even during this horror, I felt a compassion, an acceptance of my limitations by Jesus and the crowd of others.

All of a sudden in my mind from left to right like an IMAX movie, I saw all the very important moments of my life up to that present time. Most of the earlier moments in my life . . . I had long forgotten about until this happened. I had mixed feelings about this but mostly was peaceful.

I saw my childhood and felt the emotions my actions created in others. I learned that many of the things I thought I did "wrong" were not necessarily wrong. I also learned of opportunities to love others that I passed up. I learned that no matter what has been done to me, there is more to the story that my ego might not see or understand. My life has [changed] because I take into account more the feelings of others when I act.

If NDEs are real experiences, we should expect that the events seen in life reviews really happened even if some of them were forgotten. Conversely, if NDEs are not real, we can expect that there is significant error in their content and perhaps even hallucinatory features.

To explore the realness of the life review, NDERF studied the reality of the content of life reviews in NDEs. As part of this study, we looked for any content in the narratives of life reviews that appeared to be unrealistic. If unrealistic content was never or rarely found, we reasoned that the content of life reviews as a whole could be considered real.

To help determine the reality of the content of life reviews, I studied the same 617 NDEs that were discussed in chapter 4, where I reviewed these NDEs to determine the accuracy of out-of-body observations. For each NDE containing a life review, I asked, "Is there any reason to doubt, for either you personally or the experiencer, that any of the content of the scenes of [that person's] past life was real?" If *any* part of the life review appeared to contain observations that appeared unrealistic to either me or the NDErs, that case was put into the "unreal" category.

A total of 617 NDEs were studied. A life review was described in 88 NDEs (14 percent). The results of this study were convincing. *None* of the life reviews contained content that was considered unrealistic, either to the NDErs or to me.

People who had near-death experiences were often impressed that their life review contained real details of their life that they had long forgotten. For example, this man was sleeping in the backseat of a car when the driver slammed into the back of a truck. He went from sleeping to traveling up to meet a cluster of beings. The way he describes it,

The sensation was of a piece of a metal being swept into a magnet. The emotion was overwhelming, with incredible love associated with the magnetic effect. I sensed I always knew them [the beings], but when I came upon one being, I wasn't sure who it was. I left and returned to my body, which seemed as if I were putting on soiled clothes.

He was then treated to a life review in which

[e]verything in my life, including long-forgotten details, made sense.

Lisa said about her life review:

The being of light knew everything about me. It knew all I had ever thought, said, or done, and it showed me my whole life in a flash of an instant. I was shown all of the details in my life, the one I'd already lived, and all that was to come if I returned to earth. It was all there at the same time, all the details of all the cause-and-effect relations in my life, all that was good or negative, all of the effects my life on earth had had on others, and all of the effects the lives of others that had touched me had had on me.

The NDERF study makes it clear that the events seen in the NDEr's life review are real. Our finding that NDEs contain consistently realistic life reviews are further strong evidence for the reality of near-death experiences.

SKEPTICS: DEFENSE MECHANISM OR SHORT CIRCUIT

Skeptics have proposed alternative explanations for the life reviews. The two main alternative explanations are

1. the life review is a psychological defense mechanism, and
2. the life review results from the dying brain producing electrical discharges in the part of the brain responsible for memories.

Neither of these alternative explanations stands up well under scrutiny.

Dr. Susan Blackmore, a leading NDE skeptic, attributed the life review to a psychological defense mechanism at the time of a life-threatening event that involves a retreat into a timeless moment of pleasant, prior memories.[3] The explanation seems plausible until one begins encountering NDE memories that are *not* pleasant. Such content would not be expected if the life review were simply a pleasurable psychological escape from unpleasant circumstances.

Many NDEs have been reported in which the life-threatening event was sudden, unexpected, and occurred with immediate unconsciousness, such as an unanticipated car crash. The NDEs would have unconsciousness occur so rapidly that a psychological defense mechanism would not have time to develop.

And then there are NDEs and subsequent life reviews that take place under general anesthesia. No theory can explain NDEs that occur under general anesthesia because the NDErs should perceive nothing.

The second suggestion from skeptics is that the life review is only a product of a dying brain, one that is producing electrical discharges in the brain's memory centers. Writing in the magazine *Skeptical Inquirer*, Blackmore wrote: "The experience of seeing excerpts from your life flash before you is not really as mysterious as it first seems. It has long been known that stimulation of cells in the temporal lobe of the brain can produce instant experiences that seem like the reliving of memories. Also, temporal-lobe epilepsy can produce similar experiences, and such seizures can involve other limbic structures in the brain, such as the amygdala and hippocampus, which are also associated with memory."[4]

Is this really true? Let's first look at the claim that stimulation of the brain can produce prior memories similar to life reviews in NDEs or any other element of near-death experiences. "Stimulation" of the brain refers to electrical stimulation of the brain, which may be done as part of a specialized neurosurgical procedure. The brain has no sensory pain nerves in it, so the procedure is generally painless. The brain electrical stimulation studies of neurosurgeon Dr. Wilder Penfield are often quoted by skeptics as reproducing many of the elements of near-death experiences, including life reviews. Noted NDE researcher Dr. Emily Williams Kelly and her coresearchers, Bruce Greyson, MD, and Edward F. Kelly, PhD, reviewed Dr. Penfield's published reports of electrical brain stimulation and found the following:

> Most of the experiences Penfield reported in fact bore little resemblance to actual NDEs. They consisted of

hearing bits of music or singing, seeing isolated and repetitive scenes that seemed familiar and *may* [emphasis added] have been fragmentary memories, hearing voices, experiencing fear or other negative emotions, or seeing bizarre imagery that was often described as dream-like.[5]

There have been others who reported the experiences of their patients undergoing procedures similar to those used by Dr. Penfield, including electrical stimulation of the brain's temporal lobes. Drs. Kelly, Greyson, and Kelly, commenting on these further studies of electrical brain stimulation, continue:

> Subsequent studies have found similar experimental phenomena, especially fear or anxiety and fragmented, distorted experiences quite *unlike* NDE phenomenology.[6]

More recent studies by Dr. Olaf Blanke and associates suggest that they were able to produce OBE-type experiences with electrical brain stimulation.[7, 8] The first patient they reported described a purported OBE that involved seeing herself from above, but only her lower trunk and legs. She reported visual distortions, which included seeing her legs getting shorter and moving toward her face. This type of OBE with partial body visualization and hallucinatory features is essentially never reported in out-of-body experiences occurring during near-death experiences. I coauthored a paper that documented other discrepancies between the Blanke account and true OBEs.[9]

Blackmore and other skeptics have claimed that seizures, especially those associated with temporal-lobe epilepsy, can produce experiences similar to life reviews or other NDE elements. However, the evidence indicates this is not true. As neurologist Dr. Ernst Rodin stated,

> In spite of having seen hundreds of patients with temporal lobe seizures during three decades of professional life, I have never come across that symptomatology [of NDEs] as part of a seizure.[10]

Other researchers have documented that the experiences produced by electrical brain stimulation or seizures are almost always unlike any element of near-death experiences.[11] At NDERF we have case reports from epileptics who had frequent seizures but no near-death experience until an exceptionally severe seizure became a life-threatening event.

The best evidence points to the conclusion that electrical brain stimulation and seizures do not consistently reproduce *any* elements of NDE. The skeptical argument that NDEs are somehow related to electrical brain stimulation or seizures needs to be relegated to the status of urban legend.

Accurate and transformative life reviews are a hallmark of NDEs, and they point to a reality beyond what we know from our earthly existence. They provide important evidence for the reality of an afterlife.

PROOF #6: FAMILY REUNION

Every parting is a form of death, as every
reunion is a type of heaven.
—Tryon Edwards

Many near-death experiencers describe dramatic and joyous
reunions with people known to them who died long before
their near-death experience took place.

"COME HERE; HERE IS GOOD TO BE"

One such story came from a Finnish woman named Anitta,
who had a heart attack. Anitta found herself zooming up
a tunnel toward a bright light. "Someone" took her by the
arm and made her feel peaceful. Anitta's life came back to
her "like a film." As Anitta recounted on the NDERF
site:

Then I saw my father, just like he was when he lived, and he said to me, "Come here; here is good to be." I wanted to run to him, but I could not because there was a border between us. I cannot describe the border. It was like a wall that I could see through. Then I heard a dark voice that seemed to be everywhere, asking, "Who?" They meant my identity. And then [came] the words: "not yet."

. . . Then I was obliged to turn back, which I did not want, because I had such a good feeling there. Again I was in the tunnel, coming back very fast, and at the same time the pain in my body came back. I had cried, "No, no," when I was coming back to consciousness. For many days afterward I had a strange feeling, [like,] where am I? And I missed my father a lot, whom I had seen.

WHY SEEING IS BELIEVING

This NDEr, Anitta, had an experience that is representative of those in the NDERF study who encountered deceased relatives or friends during their near-death experience.

Why should seeing deceased friends or relatives be evidence of life after death? Because if NDEs were only a product of brain function, then one would expect that beings encountered during the NDE would be those most recently familiar to the NDEr. In other words, one would expect NDErs would most likely see people recalled from recent memory, such as the emergency personnel who helped them or the bank teller they had made a transaction with right before being hit by a car. Instead, they see friends and relatives who have died, in many cases people they haven't thought about in years or even decades.

The percentage of deceased individuals seen during NDEs, especially deceased blood relatives, is so high that I believe that encounters with deceased loved ones are not the random products of a frightened, confused, or dying brain but instead are a strong line of evidence for the reality of near-death experiences.

A study that best illustrates this was conducted in 2001 by Emily Williams Kelly, PhD, of the department of psychiatric medicine at the University of Virginia.[1] She compared 74 NDErs who had encounters with the deceased during their NDE with 200 NDErs who did not have awareness of deceased individuals.

The Kelly study found that 95 percent of the deceased individuals encountered were relatives, while only 5 percent were friends or acquaintances. Only 4 percent of the NDErs in the study met beings who were alive at the time of the NDE. Other studies have shown that in dreams or hallucinations, the beings encountered are much more likely to be people who are still living.

As part of the NDERF study, I reviewed NDEs that described meeting individuals known to the NDErs from their earthly life. For this part of the study, I reviewed the same group of 617 NDEs that we discussed in chapters 4 and 7. This review excluded living people seen by the NDErs only during out-of-body observations of earthly events, and familiar beings seen only during life reviews.

In our study group, 97 NDEs, or 16 percent, described meeting one or more beings familiar to them from their earthly life. Of these 97 NDEs, 13 were excluded from further analysis because the beings who were met were not described as being either alive or deceased at the time of the NDEs. Most of these excluded NDEs described grandparents and, less commonly, parents. With this information, and from the context of the NDE narratives, it is likely that the great majority, and possibly all, of the beings encountered in these 13 NDEs were deceased at the time of the NDEs. There were 84 NDEs where the beings encountered were described as being either alive or deceased at the time of the NDEs. Of these 84 NDEs, there were only 3 (4 percent) where the beings encountered were definitely alive at the time of the NDEs. In all 3 of these NDEs, only one being known to the NDErs from their earthly life was present. Two of these beings were their fathers, and one was a doctor. This remarkably low percentage of living beings encountered during the NDE is consistent with the findings of the Kelly study and is additional strong evidence for the reality of NDEs and the existence of an afterlife.

In the study group of 617 NDEs, there were 91 NDEs that described meeting beings familiar to them from their earthly life that also indicated whether these beings were direct family relatives or friends. Of these 91 NDEs, 74 (81 percent) encountered only relatives and 7 (8 percent) encountered both relatives and friends. The finding of a preponderance of deceased relatives during NDEs is similar to what Kelly found in her study.

"TALKING IN TELEPATHY"

One of the more remarkable NDEs shared with NDERF involving encounters with deceased relatives came from Brian, who was born totally deaf. At the age of thirteen he nearly drowned. Here is Brian's description of meeting his deceased family members.

I approached the boundary. No explanation was necessary for me to understand, at the age of ten, that once I cross[ed] the boundary, I could never come back—period. I was more than thrilled to cross. I intended to cross, but my ancestors over another boundary caught my attention. They were talking in telepathy, which caught my attention. I was born profoundly deaf and had all hearing family members, all of which knew sign language! I could read or communicate with about twenty ancestors of mine and others through telepathic methods. It overwhelmed me. I could not believe how many people I could telepathize with simultaneously.

Brian had been born totally deaf, so communication could take place only through sign language, lip-reading, or other visual forms of communication. Brian's amazing NDE involved communication unlike any he had encountered— telepathy. It is this type of communication, by the way, that takes place during almost all near-death experiences in which communication is described. To the best of my knowledge, Brian's NDE is the first ever reported from an individual born totally deaf.

Here are several more examples of those who encountered the deceased during their NDEs. I am including these other examples to show this element's remarkable consistency.

Christine was receiving chemotherapy for leukemia and was in her apartment. As a rare side effect, one of the chemotherapy drugs caused her heartbeat to become dangerously erratic. As it did, she had the following experience:

The first scene I remember was that I was in my apartment bedroom (where my body lay). My ceiling light was on, and my body lay near the right side of my bed. I was on the left side of my bed, not up in the air yet not on the ground either. I saw several people kneeling down around my body, so I couldn't really even see myself. The people wore dark clothing, so I'm assuming they were police. I think I saw one person with a white shirt (EMT?). While I was watching the "event" I was with two of my deceased relatives: my grandfather's cousin, Aunt Kate (who was more like a grandmother to me), and my uncle Harry. In life, these were really the only two members of my family (besides my mother) that I was close to. I loved them very, very much. I don't remember any strong emotion at all during the NDE. In fact, I felt almost emotionally detached from what was going on. I was not elated, I was not frightened or angry, etc. Just peaceful, calm, and . . . accepting. But I "knew" why Kate and Harry were there. I knew that they were going to take me somewhere.

Peter was six years old when he cut himself so severely that he "bled to death."

Then I looked to my left and saw my grandmother who had passed away when I was nine months old. I also saw all of my deceased relatives with her, thousands of them. They were in translucent spirit form.

Bob fell out of a building and landed three stories below. He suffered multiple injuries, including a brain injury. During his NDE he met many deceased relatives:

My relatives (all deceased) were there, all at their prime in life. They were dressed, I would say, 1940s style, which would have been prime years for most. Relatives I knew of, such as my grandfathers, but never knew in life were there, as well as uncles/aunts who passed before I knew them.

At times NDErs encounter beings that they believe to be alive at the time of their NDE, only to find that they were actually deceased. Here's an example of what I am talking about. Douglas's heart stopped, and he had to be defibrillated twelve times. Here's his story:

Now while all this was happening, two hundred miles away my grandfather had a heart attack at the same time. We were both kept alive through the night, but the next morning we both had heart attacks again. At that time I had my NDE. There was no tunnel of light that I hear so much about; it was just an expanse of white light.

Off in the distance to my right was what appeared to be the shadow of a large oak tree with a large group of people standing under it. As I got closer to this group I recognized the people standing in the front of the group as my grandmother, my great-uncle Glenn, my great-aunt Lala, my great-aunt Wanda, her husband, Lee, a woman that was like a grandmother to my sister and me, and then a group of people that I thought I knew but at that time I couldn't put names to their faces. I tried to speak to them, but all they would say to me is "We're not waiting for you; go home."

Then the last thing I remember from that side was my grandfather's voice. I did not see him; I just heard his voice say, "You're the luckiest boy I know."

Then three days later I awoke in the hospital with my mother and sister standing over my bed. My mother says that my first question was about the play I was working on at the time, and my second question was about my grandfather. . . . My grandfather [had] died at the same time two hundred miles away.

For another example, when a child we will call Sandra was five years old, she contracted encephalitis and lost consciousness. It was then that she encountered her neighbor. Here is a paraphrase of her story, which she shared with the NDERF site:

As I was unconscious, an elderly family friend appeared to me and said, "Go home right now." I didn't really know what he meant. I was out of my body when he appeared, and I immediately went back into my body. Before long I opened my eyes, and my family was there smiling in their great relief that I had returned from unconsciousness. When I told them that I had seen our friend and that he insisted I go home, they looked at me with great concern. The day after I went into the hospital, our friend had died of a heart attack. I did not know he had died until after I shared my experience with my parents.

Later during this same experience, Sandra encountered a sister, one who had died before she was born and that she didn't know she had. A few days after she came around, Sandra was drawing a picture of the girl she had met during her coma. When she told her parents what she was drawing, they became ashen and left the room. Later they returned and told her about the sister she never knew she had, who was struck by a car and died before she was born.

JOYOUS AND YOUTHFUL

As you may have noticed, encounters with the deceased loved ones are almost always joyous reunions, not horrifying ones like what might be seen in a ghost movie. Also, although many deceased loved ones prior to death were elderly and sometimes disfigured by arthritis or other chronic illnesses, the deceased in the near-death experience are virtually always the picture of perfect health and may appear younger—even decades younger—than they did at the time of death. Those who died as very young children may appear older. But even if the deceased appear to be a very different age than when they died, the NDEr still recognizes them.

People may encounter in their near-death experience a being who seems familiar but whose identity is unknown during the NDE. Later on, the NDEr may discover the identity of this familiar but unknown being, for instance, by looking at old family photographs.[2] Most of the time these unfamiliar beings turn out to be family members from the past. We just saw an example of this from Sandra, who encountered during her NDE a sister she did not know she had. Here is another example from the NDERF site, regarding a woman we'll call Missy.

Missy suffered head trauma in an automobile accident. Although she suffered loss of memory, Missy remembers well going up a tunnel and seeing her sister. To paraphrase her story:

I saw a child that I recognized as a sister of mine who had died in a fire. I was only a year or so when she died, but I knew it was her. She had a strong family resemblance. Much later, when I was older, I confirmed it was my sister when I saw pictures of her in the family photo album.

MYSTICAL BEINGS

Sometimes NDErs meet beings who are unfamiliar; many such beings encountered by those in the NDERF study had a mystical quality. Despite being unfamiliar, these mystical beings were generally described as very loving in their interaction with the NDErs. To the question, "Did you seem to encounter a mystical being or presence?" NDErs responded with 49.9 percent selecting "Definite being, or voice clearly of mystical or otherworldly origin," while 9.8 percent selected "Unidentifiable voice," and 40.3 percent selected "Neither." Here are some examples of the mystical beings they encountered.

Jonathan was told he had only a 1 percent chance of surviving surgery on his esophagus.

[I] remember standing about ten feet up and ten feet to the side of my body on the [operating] table. A person was standing next to me, but I didn't look at him/her. I had no fear or questions to ask;

I just observed. Around the table were at least a dozen nurses and doctors. But what was so emotional was the presence of [glowing] people that I can only describe as angels. Each angel was guiding the hands of the staff they were standing next to. I heard no noise, no voices, no music. It was peacefully quiet. I don't remember details too specific, such as what tools were used or the exact position of my body, but only because I was focused so much on the angels guiding the staff in everything they did, from walking to the use of the tools within my chest cavity. Even after the operation, I still had an unusual peace and no fear. The doctor said it was the best operation he had ever gone through—there were no problems at all—and he was impressed at my rate of recovery.

Andrew suffered an allergic reaction that left him unconscious. He wrote,

I was aware of another person or being; it was feminine, and she spoke to me. It was a feeling of presence, not really seeing. She told me everything would be all right and that [when I thought about having so much knowledge] I would know the secrets of the universe.

Jesse overdosed on a mixture of heroin and cocaine, calling it "an instant death." During his NDE,

I met this being filled with love, joy, patience, compassion who knew my thoughts and knew everything I've ever done in this life and beyond! He also knew and remembered who I am!

A man we'll call Leonard had a heart attack. He described 360-degree vision as he watched the frantic efforts to resuscitate him:

On the other side communication is done via telepathy (thought transfer). I must tell you that God has a fantastic sense of humor; I never laughed so much in all my life!

During a near-death experience, these mystical beings may be sensed or heard but not actually seen. When mystical beings are seen, their appearance is variable. Some in the NDERF study described these beings as angels. They usually don't have wings. Rather, they may appear similar to earthly beings, or they may be described as beings of light, without easily definable features.

Communication with these mystical beings, as with known deceased beings, is almost always telepathic. Mystical beings may be present at any time during the NDE. They often are present at a time of discussion near the end of the NDE.

The NDERF study's conclusions—that NDErs see deceased relatives and friends during their experience—is supported by Emily Williams Kelly's previously cited study. As noted, her research found that 95 percent of the deceased individuals encountered were relatives, and only 5 percent were friends or acquaintances. The age of the NDEr did not make any difference in whether or not they encountered a deceased being. If the deceased relatives encountered during NDEs were only a product of earthly memory, it would be expected that older individuals, who would have experienced more deaths of people that they knew in their lifetimes, would encounter more deceased relatives. However, this is not what the Kelly study found.

It might also be expected that NDErs would encounter deceased individuals that they were emotionally close to.

Once again, though, Kelly's study held a surprise. For 32 percent of the deceased beings encountered, the NDErs were emotionally neutral to or distant from the beings or had never previously met them. The NDErs in the study frequently commented that the individuals they encountered were completely unexpected.[3]

"THE STARLIT STRIP"

No skeptic's argument can explain the overwhelming percentage of deceased beings encountered during NDEs, especially given that living beings would be much more likely to occupy a place in the NDErs' recent memory. People who undergo near-death experiences are generally not thinking about the deceased at the time of their NDEs, anyway. Yet people who died years or decades before are commonly encountered. The skeptics' suggestion that NDErs expect to see these deceased beings cannot explain NDEs in which the NDEr had never met the deceased or did not even know the person was deceased at the time of the NDE.

The findings of the NDERF study and others are consistent with what NDErs themselves generally believe: they are briefly reunited with deceased relatives and friends when they venture to the other side.

Reuniting with our lost loved ones is the reality—not just the hope—of the NDE. As Mark Twain said, "Death is the starlit strip between the companionship of yesterday and the reunion of tomorrow." It is the convincing stories collected in the NDERF website that lead me to believe these reunions are real and strong evidence of the afterlife.

PROOF #7: FROM
THE MOUTHS OF BABES

Life, like a child, laughs, shaking its rattle of death as it runs.
—Indian poet Rabindranath Tagore

Skeptics have suggested that Oprah created the near-death experience. They say this with tongue in cheek, of course (or so I think). What they are jokingly suggesting is that Oprah and other cultural icons have popularized the near-death experience to such a point that people claim to have NDEs when they really don't. It is hip to have NDEs, the skeptics claim, and people will go to any length to fit into that category.

Frankly, fabricated NDEs are more rare than the skeptics would have you believe. I have run into fewer than ten NDEs shared on the NDERF survey form that were definitely fabricated—out of 1,300 NDEs shared with NDERF. But still the skeptical questions remain: Has our culture become so familiar with near-death experiences that people are now embellishing their experiences? Or, worse, are they creating them out of whole cloth?

The short answer to those questions is no. The fact that NDEs have been the subject of many television shows and a couple of feature films does not mean that people are now pretending to have NDEs.

Still there are skeptics. Carol Zaleski, a Harvard-trained theologian, describes NDEs as a product of "religious imagination."[1] *The Skeptic's Dictionary* says, "NDE stories are now known to a large audience. Thus, when new stories are told about going into the light, etc., one has to be concerned that these stories may have been contaminated. They may reflect what one has heard and what one expects."[2] And, at the far end of skepticism come those who think that NDEs are the work of Satan.

Personally, I think all of the above are wrong. If asked why, I have many answers, and one of them is: "The children told me."

It is through young children that we can help determine if NDEs are just a made-up phenomenon. And it's through very young children that we can help prove once and for all that NDEs are natural events, not events made up or influenced to match some television program.

Let's look at some of the data from the NDERF study to see how the NDEs of very young children relate to the subject of NDEs overall. For the sake of categorizing, I call children five years of age and younger "very young children." Most five-year-olds have not yet started elementary school, where cultural influences are accelerated. A child of five or younger is less likely to have experienced the cultural influences that might affect how they interpret a near-death experience. Plus, very young children have less-developed views of death than older children and adults. It is unlikely that very young children have heard of near-death experiences or that they understand NDEs even if they have.

In essence, very young children are practically a blank slate when it comes to the subject of death, which makes them an important subject group to use when studying near-death experiences.

In prior chapters responses were presented to survey questions from the NDERF study of 613 NDErs, all with NDE Scale scores of 7 and higher. To compare the content of NDEs of very young children to older children and adults, I used this same group of 613 NDErs, minus 2 NDErs who did not give their age at the time of their NDE on the NDERF survey. I used the same methodology that was previously described in chapter 6, where NDEs occurring under general anesthesia were compared to all other NDEs.

This study included 26 NDErs age 5 and below (average age 3.6 years old) and 585 NDErs age 6 and above at the time of their NDEs. The survey consisted of thirty-three questions that addressed the content of NDEs. We compared the responses to these thirty-three questions between the two groups.

The results: Very young children had every NDE element that older children and adults had. There was no statistically significant difference in the responses to any of the thirty-three survey questions regarding the content of the NDEs between very young children and older children and adults. There were only two questions with a trend toward a statistically different response between the two groups.

One of these questions was "Did time seem to speed up?"

There were three possible responses to this question: "Everything seemed to be happening all at once," "Time seemed to go faster than usual," and "Neither." Very young children were somewhat more likely to select the "Neither" option in response to this question. However, there were no differences between the two groups in response to the more generally worded survey question "Did you have any sense of altered space or time?"

The other question with a trend toward a statistically significant difference in the responses between the two groups was "Were your senses more vivid than usual?" The three possible responses to this question were "Incredibly more so," "More so than usual," and "Neither." Very young children were somewhat more likely to select the "More so than usual" option. However, there were no differences between the two groups to three more specifically worded questions that addressed their senses during the NDEs. These three questions with no differences in responses between the two groups asked "How did your highest level of consciousness and alertness during the experience compare to your normal everyday consciousness and alertness?" and two questions asking if their vision and hearing during their NDEs differed from everyday vision and hearing.

The conclusion: Very young children have every NDE element that older children and adults have in their NDEs. This group of 26 very young children, age 5 and below, appears to have NDE content that is identical to that of older children and adult NDEs. The percentage of time NDE elements occur during their NDEs is not statistically different between the two groups for any of the NDE elements. The two questions with only a trend toward statistical significance are not corroborated by differences in responses to other questions asking about the same NDE elements.

Dr. Cherie Sutherland, a noted NDE researcher, reviewed thirty years of scholarly literature regarding NDEs in children, including very young children. Here's what Dr. Sutherland has to say about NDEs in very young children:

> It has often been supposed that the NDEs of very young children will have a content limited to their vocabulary. However, it is now clear that the age of children at the time of their NDE does not in any way determine its complexity. Even prelinguistic children have later reported quite complex experiences. . . . Age does not seem in any way to affect the content of the NDE.[3]

I agree with Dr. Sutherland. The NDERF study is by far the largest study of NDEs in very young children ever published. We may now be more confident than ever in concluding that the content of NDEs in very young children is not affected by their young age at the time of their NDEs.[4]

There is much more to understanding near-death experiences than simply analyzing responses to questions with statistics. There is no substitute for *reading* NDEs to see for yourself their deeper dimension. I have read every NDE ever shared with NDERF. In reading the NDEs of very young children, I see that their thinking may be childlike during the NDE. However, I also see a deeper dimension of their NDEs that goes beyond even the very detailed NDERF survey questions. There is a subjective similarity between the NDEs of children of all ages and adults that can only be appreciated by reading the accounts.

What about older children? Do they have the same NDE content as adults? It is difficult to select the age that separates children from adults. Eighteen years old is a legal definition of adulthood in many countries. However, youth between the ages of sixteen and eighteen are able to drive, often start employed jobs, and frequently begin romantic relationships. I consider those between sixteen and eighteen years old to be between childhood and adulthood rather than to be children. With this consideration, I defined *children* to be younger than sixteen years old and *adults* to be age sixteen and older.

Using the same methodology I used to study the content of NDEs in the very young, the content of the NDEs of 133 children and 478 adults were compared.

The results: The responses to the thirty-three questions about NDE content were reviewed. There was only one question that had a statistically different response between the two groups. This question asked, "Did you see a light?" Children were more likely to answer "Yes" and less likely to answer "No." A similarly worded question asked, "Did you see or feel surrounded by a brilliant light?" Possible responses included "Light clearly of mystical or otherworldly origin," "Unusually bright light," and "Neither." I believe this latter question, one of the NDE Scale questions, better addresses the mystical, unearthly light that NDErs often encounter. There was no statistical difference between children and adults in their response to this question.

The conclusion: This group of 133 children, age fifteen and below, appears to have NDE content that is identical to that of adult NDEs. Considering the above discussion, there does not appear to be any statistical difference between the two groups in the percentage of occurrence of each NDE element during their NDEs.

As with the NDEs in very young children, this is the largest study ever published that directly compares the content of childhood and adult NDEs. I coauthored a book chapter that included a review of thirty years of scholarly research on childhood NDEs. That chapter was written before we had the results available from the NDERF study of childhood NDEs. From prior published scholarly literature, we could still conclude:

> Over the first three decades of NDE research, investigators have published findings on several hundred childhood NDEs. NDEs in children appear to be accurately remembered, even if shared years later in adulthood. The contents of children's NDEs appear similar to those of adults and do not appear to be substantially affected by age.[5]

The NDEs of children, even very young children, have the same content as adult NDEs. This strongly suggests that NDEs are not significantly influenced by preexisting cultural influences, beliefs, or life experiences. This is further powerful evidence that NDEs, and their consistent indication of an afterlife, are real.

Below are several case studies from very young children (five years old and younger) and children over five. Note their similarity.

CHILDREN'S NDEs

Five-year-old Paul was returning home from getting his school uniform tailored when he dashed into the road and was struck by a passing van:

I jumped from the Jeep and ran to cross the road to reach home first. What I remember is something coming beside me (later I knew it was a van). What I really remember is just [taking] one or two steps into the road before something happened. . . . I felt like a hydrogen balloon floating in the air. I was going upward. I slowly opened my eyes, and I saw my body lying on the roadside. I got really frightened. I felt . . . paralyzed and I was going upward, but I felt . . . someone was carrying me very lovingly (an unconditional love). I tried to move my body and turned my eyes upward to see who was carrying me. What I saw was Mother Mary. She wore a blue and pink dress with a crown. . . . I felt very comfortable in her hands.

When she was eleven years old Jennifer was in a severe car accident. She saw her "limp and lifeless body" below. The voice of a spiritual being told her she was needed back at the accident site to help the unconscious driver. Here is her experience as she wrote it:

Then the voice said, "His nose is cut off his face; you will need to go back and help him; he is bleeding to death." I said, "No, let somebody else do it. He will be fine without my help. I do not want to go back down there. No!" The voice said, "I will tell you what to do. You take off his shirt after you pick his nose up off the floorboard of the car. It will be next to your feet and his right foot. Place his nose on his face, pressing down to stop the bleeding. It's just blood, so do not be afraid. I am with you as always." (I knew I was never alone from as far back as I could remember.) "So then, Jennifer, you will begin to walk him up the right side of the road, and a car will come. Tell the man to take you to the nearest hospital. Keep the man calm, and lead him to the hospital where you were born. You know the way and everything will be all right. You must do this. Understand?"

Jennifer goes on to say that when she returned to her body everything happened as she was told by the spiritual being. A car stopped and carried them to the hospital where she was born. She was able to calm both the anxious driver and the accident victim who lost his nose. And there was a happy ending: a skin graft was used to reattach the nose with "barely a scratch left to notice." The astonished emergency room doctor said, "I cannot explain what kind of miracle I just witnessed in this emergency room today."

AGELESS CONSISTENCY

I want to be the first to point out that many of the children's NDEs you just read were reported many years or even decades after they took place. Skeptics may say that children are not likely to remember NDEs that happened so long ago and therefore are not able to accurately report what truly happened.

William Serdahely, PhD, addressed these skeptical concerns. Serdahely, a health sciences professor from Montana

State University, compared five NDEs reported by children with five NDEs that occurred in childhood and were reported years later when the NDErs were adults. He analyzed the reports by comparing forty-seven characteristics of NDEs between the two groups. Serdahely concluded, "This study . . . supports the claims of previous researchers that adults' retrospective reports of childhood NDEs are not embellished or distorted."[6]

Another study, this by Bruce Greyson, MD, in 2007 found that NDEs do not seem embellished or diminished even after nearly twenty years.[7] This was a study of seventy-two NDErs who shared their NDEs and answered the sixteen questions comprising the NDE Scale in the 1980s and then answered the questions again almost twenty years later. Comparison of the two administrations of the scale showed no significant differences in overall scale scores or in responses to any of the sixteen questions. This study provides some of the strongest evidence that NDEs are reliably remembered even when shared decades after their occurrence.

An additional important study was done by Pim van Lommel, MD, and associates in 2001.[8] This was the largest prospective study of NDEs ever performed. As part of this study, NDErs who suffered cardiac arrest were interviewed about the NDE shortly after the incident, then two and eight years later. This study found that NDErs accurately recalled their NDEs eight years after their occurrence.

It doesn't matter if the NDEr is four years old or forty-four, the elements of the near-death experience remain the same. The best evidence finds that NDEs are neither embellished nor forgotten over time. NDEs are not "created" in the subject's mind by what they see on television or read in books, and they are not significantly modified by cultural influences. Near-death experiences are *real* events that happen to people of all ages.

What do the children who approach death think of their experience on the other side, and what do they do with it over the course of their lives? The Transformations Study conducted by Dr. Morse provides evidence that NDEs create changes in an individual that can't be faked.[9] He studied more than four hundred people, some of whom had near-death experiences and some who did not. He administered tests with questions about happiness, spirituality, death anxiety, mysticism, materialism, eating habits, and psychic abilities. All of this was aimed at exploring the aftereffects of NDEs on people who'd experienced them as children.

Morse found that those who'd had near-death experiences as children had less death anxiety than the non-NDE population; they also had increased psychic abilities, a higher zest for life, and increased intelligence. Among his conclusions was that NDEs are real because their long-term effects are real. In short, as we at NDERF say, *you can't fake the effects of a near-death experience.*

REAL AND TRANSFORMING

All of which reminds me of Katie, who as a three-year-old child inhaled a cashew nut that lodged in her windpipe. She was standing in the kitchen when the shocking event took place. She turned blue and passed out. Her grandfather, a firefighter, was unable to revive her and pronounced her dead.

The ambulance arrived nearly thirty minutes after the 911 call. Katie was watching much of the action from a place outside of her body. As she wrote:

When I died, I rose above my body and saw my grandfather working on my body. My body was of no interest to me; instead, I moved out of the room toward a presence I felt in the living room area. I went toward this presence, which was within a brilliant, sun[lit], bright, space—not a tunnel, but an area. The presence was unbelievable peace, love, acceptance, calm, and joy. The presence enveloped me, and my joy was indescribable—as I write this I am brought back to this emotion, and it delights me still. The feeling is spectacular. I did not experience this presence as God (I was too young to understand the concept), but I did experience this presence as that which made me. I knew without a doubt that I was a made creature, a being that owed its existence to this presence.

I do not remember reentering my body.

When I woke up the next day, I knew two things for sure: (1) that there is life after death and (2) I was a created being. I did not know this as rational knowledge, but rather I expressed this by pestering my mother with question after question: Who made me? What was eternity? And what was God? She was unable to answer my questions but was wise enough to let me talk to others who could.

In her NDERF entry, Katie declares several times that the experience was "definitely real."

Even now, when I recall the experience, it is more real than anything I have ever experienced in my life. I recall not only the memory but also the emotion. This still motivates me to ask questions.

A skeptic could still discount these as just being empty words. But NDErs often *actively* respond to their remarkable experience. Katie's NDE motivated her to continue her search into her adult life:

This experience moved me so deeply that I have dedicated my life to looking for answers to my questions through the study [of] both philosophy and religion. I am currently working on [a] doctorate in theology.

Near-death experiences are real and transformative. They are not the product of our television culture, and they are not invented by the people who experience them, even if those people are children.

Personally, I listen to children more carefully now than ever before. From the mouths of children we can learn important lessons pointing to the reality of the afterlife.

PROOF #8: WORLDWIDE CONSISTENCY

Man is a piece of the universe made alive.
—Ralph Waldo Emerson

Ours is the largest cross-cultural study of NDEs ever performed, a fact that makes me feel confident in presenting these remarkable conclusions:

- *The core NDE experience is the same all over the world:* Whether it's a near-death experience of a Hindu in India, a Muslim in Egypt, or a Christian in the United States, the same core elements are present in all, including out-of-body experience, tunnel experience, feelings of peace, beings of light, a life review, reluctance to return, and transformation after the NDE. In short, the experience of dying appears similar among all humans, no matter where they live.

- *Preexisting cultural beliefs do not significantly influence the content of NDEs:* Near-death experiences from around the world appear to have similar content regardless of the culture of the country that the NDErs live in. This is certainly consistent with our findings in chapter 9 that very young children, age five and younger, who have received much less cultural influence than adults, have NDEs with content that is the same as that of older children and adults. Near-death experiences occurring under general anesthesia can't have any cultural influence, or influence from any other prior experiences in their life. However, NDEs occurring under general anesthesia are basically the same as all other NDEs, as we saw in chapter 6.

The striking ability of near-death experiencers to consistently recall in great detail their experiences, even decades later, is a testament to the power of the near-death experience. It is a unique and remarkable state of consciousness. It is often the most dramatic and transformative experience in the life of NDErs, wherever in the world they live.

The evidence suggesting that there is no significant difference in near-death experiences worldwide makes possible a major step forward in human relations. It means that at the point of death, *all* people may have a similar experience. We may be separated by languages and cultures, but the possibility of having similar spiritual experiences as dramatic and transformative as NDEs unites us around the world.

Recognizing that people from all cultures experience similar events at the point of death may be a useful tool for cross-cultural understanding and dialogue. That makes NDEs an important spiritual concept that can help humanity strive toward world peace. The evidence that near-death experiences are basically the same *worldwide* may be a reason to stop bickering over differences and instead focus on our similarities.

LARGEST CROSS-CULTURAL STUDY EVER

Some years ago Jody Long began the enormous project of translating the NDERF survey into non-English languages. Jody began developing a network of volunteer language translators, one that has grown to more than two hundred fifty translators worldwide. These volunteers translate non-English NDEs, all of which are posted on the website in both their original language and the English translation. The volunteers also translate English NDEs posted on NDERF into non-English languages. This allows bilingual readers to correct any possible inaccurate translations. Currently there are more than two thousand near-death-experience accounts in non-English languages posted on NDERF, with more added regularly.

Sections of the NDERF website and the NDEr questionnaire have been translated into over twenty languages. With the NDERF questionnaire translated into so many different languages, nearly all NDErs throughout the world can find the NDERF questionnaire in a language they are familiar with. This allows NDERF to receive NDEs from around the world, including non-English NDEs. No prior study has been able to directly compare so many NDEs shared in English with NDEs shared in languages other than English by having all the NDErs personally answer the same questions. That was done by using the questionnaires on the NDERF website.

For the NDERF cross-cultural study, NDEs from countries where English is not the predominant language were divided into two study groups. The first study group included 79 NDEs shared in languages other than English, and the second study group included 26 NDEs shared in English from countries where English was not the predominant language. The NDERF study also looked at NDEs from non-Western countries, which will be discussed later.

The first study group was 79 NDErs from countries where English is not the predominant language who shared their NDEs in a language other than English. The comparison group included 583 NDEs shared in English from countries where English is the predominant language.

To compare the two groups of NDEs, I used nearly the same methodology that was discussed previously in chapters 6 and 9, where we discussed the NDEs under general anesthesia and in children. For the cross-cultural part of the NDERF study, I included all NDEs regardless of their score on the NDE Scale. I felt this was reasonable, as the NDE Scale has not been validated for non-English NDEs and non-Western NDEs. This part of the study included only NDEs that were posted on the NDERF website.

The results: In comparing the first study group composed of non-English-language NDEs with the comparison group, all thirty-three NDE elements were present in both groups. Of the thirty-three NDE elements compared, eleven elements appeared with a statistically differing frequency of occurrence between the two groups, and two more elements were borderline statistically different. These results indicate many significant differences in the responses of these two groups of NDErs to the thirty-three questions about NDE content.

The results were surprising and puzzling. Could these results be due to NDEs being different around the world? Or could language translation issues result in them seeming to have different content when their content is actually similar?

In scientific studies, when puzzling results are found, it often helps to look deeper for an explanation. That is exactly what we did with the NDERF cross-cultural study. To look deeper at non-English NDEs, an experienced NDE research volunteer, Lynn, came to the rescue. A questionnaire was developed for reviewing the content of NDEs posted on NDERF. The questionnaire included fifteen questions about NDE content. All 79 non-English NDEs in the first study group had been translated into English and posted on the NDERF website. Lynn completed this questionnaire for all 79 non-English NDEs and all 583 English NDEs in the comparison group. Her hard work allowed us to more directly compare the content of non-English NDEs with the comparison group of English-language NDEs.

From the comparison of fifteen NDE elements between the two groups, there were only two questions where the percentage of occurrence of the NDE element was statistically different. There were no NDE elements where the percentage of occurrence of the NDE element was borderline statistically different.

Lynn's review of both groups of near-death-experience accounts found many fewer differences in NDE content than was suggested from the previous results from the first study group. This suggested to me that non-English-speaking NDErs might have a somewhat different interpretation and understanding of the translated NDERF survey questions than did English-speaking NDErs. This language barrier might account for most, and perhaps all, of the apparent differences in responses to the NDERF survey questions between the two groups.

It is very likely that some words and concepts in the NDERF survey questions may be misunderstood if the survey is taken in a language other than English. For example, the NDERF survey includes words and phrases like *senses, unearthly,* and *harmony or unity with the universe.* These words and phrases were not haphazardly chosen. They are straight from the NDE Scale questions, the most validated questionnaire for *English-language* NDE surveys. However, if you don't know the nuances of English, it is easy to see how these words and phrases could be misunderstood or interpreted differently from their English meanings.

To help understand how language barriers might affect responses to the NDERF survey, the NDERF cross-cultural study looked at a second study group. The second study group was made up of 26 NDEs that had been shared with NDERF in English but that came from countries around the world where English is not the prevailing language. This is an interesting study group, as these NDErs live in a culture unique to their country yet understand English well enough to share their NDEs and complete a complex questionnaire in English. The comparison group included the same 583 NDEs used in the first study group, that is, NDEs shared in English from countries where English is the predominant language. As with the first study group, I compared the responses of the second study group with the comparison group to the thirty-three questions on the NDERF questionnaire that covered NDE elements.

I almost fell out of my chair when I first saw the results of this part of the study. All thirty-three NDE elements were present in both groups. The percentage of NDEs with each NDE element was the same in both groups; no NDE element occurred statistically significantly more or less often in either group. There was a trend toward a significant difference in the responses to only one question.

The conclusion: The most reasonable conclusion from the NDERF cross-cultural NDE study is that the content of near-death experiences appears to be the same around the world. Such experiences, in both English- and non-English-speaking countries, include the same NDE elements. The elements appear to follow the same order of occurrence. In reading the accounts of NDEs from around the world, including those shared in English and those translated into English, I am impressed at how strikingly similar they are. You have probably noted that in prior chapters there are many examples of NDEs from around the world, and these experiences were like all other NDEs. There appears to be little difference, and most likely no difference, in the frequency of occurrence of NDE elements in NDEs around the world. This is further strong evidence that NDEs are not products of cultural beliefs or prior life experiences. Near-death experiences are, in a word, *real*.

MORE THAN JUST YES AND NO

Comparing NDEs from different cultures will always require more than just statistics. As we have seen throughout this book, NDEs often have an emotion, a power, and a depth that transcend the limited questions typically asked to "understand" them. Questions that require a "Yes," "Uncertain," or "No" response simply don't do justice to this experience. I believe that to *really* understand NDEs, one must read them.

To understand my position that NDEs around the world are more similar than dissimilar, it is helpful to read some representative NDEs that were shared in languages other than English and then translated into English. I find them similar to typical NDEs from English-speaking countries.

Elisa from Italy was transformed so much by this NDE, which took place when she fell from a cliff into a ravine, that she considers it her "second birth":

Suddenly I slid from the wall, and then all was dark around me, deep dark. I didn't have a body, I was immaterial. . . . I forgot my body. The time moved fast, and my thoughts were very fast. I saw myself at two years old, then at four in the sea, etc. Suddenly my life was over, and then I saw three sides of my probable future. In that moment I was very sad because I was dead and I knew it clearly and I wanted to return. . . . Slowly I saw a bright light around me; per instinct I [knew] that was "the line," the "passage," and if I passed through it I was dead. I decided not to pass into it because I wanted to live in my world and enjoy all things in it. . . . I began to pray. . . . Suddenly it was dark but a different dark, and I began to feel my own body again, and then I opened my eyes and saw the blue sky, and I was ecstatic because I returned in life. I was completely changed.

A woman we will call Hafur, from Colombia, had a near-death experience that allowed her to see her life reviewed several times. It gave her insight into what was important in her life:

The figure on my right, who was guiding me, stopped, and I could not see his face, and as though we were at a small, enclosed beach, there was a hill that served as a place for projecting my life from beginning to end several times, at first rapidly and afterward more slowly. It was amazing how my life was shown with events I had completely forgotten about and others that were so insignificant that it felt like I was seeing each frame of the personal movie of my life on earth. I realized that I understood everything with a great clarity and superlucidity I had never experienced before. I discovered that I had personally chosen to take on a physical body and have the life experiences I was having. I realized I had wasted time in suffering, and what I should have been doing was using my freedom to choose true love, and not pain, in all that came into my life.

DIFFERENT INTERPRETATION

As you can see, these experiences have the same elements as NDEs from people in Nebraska or New York. And although there may be some minor differences, in truth, looking at NDEs around the world is like showing a class of young, multinational students a photograph of the Eiffel Tower in France; some will know what it is, others will think it's scaffolding for a building in progress, and others will think it's a spaceship. All of the children are seeing the same thing; they are just interpreting and expressing it differently based on what they know of life.

One need only read several of these incredible accounts to realize that there is a raw power in NDEs that transcends language. There are so many examples of this that I could easily fill a book with nothing but transformative near-death experiences from all over the world. But if I had to choose just one that sums up the message of all NDEs worldwide, it might be that of Hafur, the woman from Colombia whose experience is quoted above. Her experience allowed her to see her life several times, as though "I was seeing each frame of the personal movie of my life on earth."

This experience reshaped Hafur, providing her with revelations that transcend geographic and language barriers. Below is an edited version of the wisdom she received from the light and that she included on her NDERF questionnaire when completing this sentence: A part of what I understood and remember today is . . .

- We live in a "plural unity" or "oneness." In other words, our reality is "unity in plurality and plurality in unity."
- That I was everything and everything was me, without essential differences other than in earthly appearances.
- That there is no God outside ourselves, but rather, God is in everything and everything is a part of God, as is life itself.

- That everything is part of an essential game of life itself, and to that degree we live by true love—unconditional and universal.
- That everything is experience and that this life and the next are essentially the same because everything is God.
- Death is a metamorphosis of time—one more illusion born of our mental concepts.
- That "I" includes "we."
- That the "creator" is eternally creating, and one of the creations is the practice of conscious love. One learns to paint by painting.
- Consciously living by love is the essence of life itself.

At the end of Hafur's list, she expressed a frustration that I have read and heard from many near-death experiencers. "I learned thousands of other things without end," she wrote. "It is difficult to express in words because words are insufficient."

Perhaps that's another real issue. It isn't just words that get in the way. It's the indescribable quality of the near-death experience that we are often wrestling with. That alone makes it a universal experience.

So far we have looked at near-death experiences from around the world. Some of these NDE accounts came from non-Western countries with cultures that are usually very different from the cultures of English-speaking countries. We will take a closer look at these fascinating NDEs from non-Western countries.

NON-WESTERN NEAR-DEATH EXPERIENCES

Next we will look at near-death experiences in non-Western countries. I consider a "non-Western country" to include areas of the world that are predominantly not of Jewish or Christian heritage.[1] Near-death experiences from people living in non-Western countries are *much* harder to study than are those of their Western counterparts. Researchers encounter both geographical and language barriers in reaching non-Western NDErs. Some people who had near-death experiences have difficulty describing their experience in words, and a language barrier may compound this problem.[2] Finally, people living in non-Western countries may not have been exposed to the concept of near-death experience. They may have had a near-death experience but not know that what they experienced is called an NDE. It is easier for the public in Western countries to hear about near-death experiences because books and the media have been discussing NDEs for decades.

A review of prior scholarly research on non-Western NDEs reveals that there is much work to be done. In the early years of researching near-death experiences, a common problem was the tendency to draw conclusions from studying small numbers of NDEs. A number of studies tried to draw conclusions from fewer than five case studies. Indeed, several of these studies attempted to draw meaningful conclusions from only one NDE case study! Drawing conclusions from a study of very few NDEs would be like testing a new medication on only a handful of people; in all likelihood very little usable information could come from such work. Over the years, as more NDEs became available for research, these earlier conclusions were frequently found to be incorrect.

In other non-Western NDE studies, some in the study group did not have convincing life-threatening events. Rather, many of these studies reported cases of apparent hallucinations, spontaneous out-of-body experiences, or other paranormal events that may happen without approaching death. Some of the people in these studies were likely undergoing febrile hallucinations, for instance, which are caused by high fever and which may be more common in countries that have more infectious illnesses.

In essence, the researchers may have believed that all the people in their study groups had had life-threatening events when they actually had not. Also, there are many non-Western NDE studies in which the definition of *near-death experience* was never made clear.

Other non-Western NDE studies used accounts that were published in the popular literature of that country. These NDEs are probably not representative of all NDEs in the country. Many of these non-Western NDE studies also relied on second-person reporting. This means that the researcher did not talk directly with the NDEr but instead talked with someone else who heard the near-death experience account, which creates the concern that there may be significant inaccuracy. Because of this concern, the NDERF study excluded all second-person near-death experiences from statistical analysis.

It is also important to realize that virtually all non-Western NDE accounts published in English had to be translated into English. This raises another concern: how accurate is the translation? Some non-English words and concepts don't translate well, and the language problem may be compounded in cultures where the topic of death is taboo. We have already seen how problematic language barriers are from our study of NDEs around the world.

I could go on and on, but my point is clear: most prior studies of non-Western NDEs have serious flaws that could create the impression that non-Western NDEs are different from Western NDEs. Let's look at some non-Western near-death experiences.

Gülden, a Muslim man from Turkey, took this voyage to a heavenly realm when an artery burst in the right temporal lobe of his brain. Here's his story:

I felt that I was rising up above my bed, in the direction of a white, very bright light. Meanwhile, I saw my uncle, who had died one month before. While passing me, he said, "Not yet." I was surprised how I understood him without spoken words, but I felt very peaceful. Later a woman came to me. If I saw her now, I would recognize her. She took me to a wonderful place with mountains and said that this was the place of my life. The place we went was beautiful, but I said to her that this place is not my life's place. Then we came to a seashore with a little village, and she said again that this place was my life, but I didn't know this place and I said to her that this is not the place of my life. After we traveled to some more very beautiful places she said that I was not ready to stay in these places and asked me what I remember about my life.

Mustapha was twelve years old and living in Algeria when he nearly drowned:

I knew that I was drowning, especially as I could not avoid swallowing seawater. Then all of a sudden I could see myself floating within the water, in an incredible calmness and physical and psychological relaxation. I could see this body, very calm, drifting slowly, and also saw bubbles coming out of its mouth. The scene was very real, but with an intense luminosity. I could see everything under the water, as if I had a diving mask on. My vision was near 300 degrees. It was like being a short distance from my body, but I could also see what was happening behind me. I noticed small details: pebbles that were ochre-colored (like fragments of house tiles), also light-colored and striped pebbles, on the seabed, seaweed floating beneath the surface. The rest was sand. There were also small, almost translucent fish just under the surface, which were moving then disappeared with a sudden flick of the tail.

Carol is from Saudi Arabia. She had a complication of childbirth. This experience, she said, helped her realize that "God is everywhere, even the smallest part of material creation." Here is her story:

I began seeing everything white around me, like this blank page to write on. At the same time I felt a presence, as if someone was with me and was explaining to me about some doubts I had at one time. Not with words, but with images and perhaps telepathy, since I do not remember hearing a voice. But I could understand everything he said, and it was all so clear and obvious that I wondered how I could not have understood this before and that my mother would also be happy to know it. I understood that everything good and bad happened for a purpose.

At NDERF we have received many accounts of near-death experiences that were personally experienced by doctors and scientists. Here is one such case. Dr. Sahar is a physician in Sudan, and here is her account:

The next day in the afternoon, I felt that pain again. I was getting worse and worse, like the delivery pain. I then fainted. My husband, who is a doctor too, hit my face quickly. I awoke at once. He hurriedly carried me to the hospital again. There they told me that my baby is out of the womb and the fallopian tube exploded, which caused me to hemorrhage. They did an urgent operation. After the operation I told my husband that I felt a very great feeling in my first faint at home. I felt that I went to another place where there is very good weather with a lovely breeze. I felt there . . . a calm and peace which I have never experienced in my life. I told him that I was talking with anonymous people for a long time, as if for months. I don't remember what we were talking about or who they were, but I remember that I was so happy with them, as if we were sitting there for months! I felt very angry and sorry when my husband made me return to consciousness. Coming back, I felt this life is narrow, dirty, and disgusting. I want to go back there and stay forever.

Simran is from India. He nearly died in a bus crash in which he experienced severe trauma, including head injuries. To Simran, one of the most meaningful parts of his near-death experience was the following:

Then a bright light appeared, having a soft man's voice that told me, "You will leave everything behind—your loved ones, the hard-earned award, money, even your clothes. You'll come to me empty-handed." The light also gave me an important message to follow it as much [as] possible.

Portions of the NDERF website have been translated into many languages, including Arabic, Chinese, Indonesian, and many others. This allows near-death experiencers from non-Western countries to share their NDEs in their own language and to respond to the same survey questions as other NDErs around the world.

The NDERF study of non-Western NDEs is unique. No prior large study has published the narratives of the NDEs, has included only experiences that were medically determined to have included a life-threatening event, and has directly compared the responses from NDErs from non-Western and Western countries to the same detailed questions about the content of their NDEs.

Nineteen non-Western NDErs shared a narrative of their near-death experience and completed the NDERF survey. Nine of these NDEs were shared in English and ten in languages other than English. We compared responses to thirty-three questions regarding NDE elements from these non-Western NDEs to the responses from the same comparison group of English NDEs from predominantly English-speaking countries that we discussed earlier in this chapter.

The results: All NDE elements that were present in Western NDEs were present in non-Western NDEs. Of the thirty-three NDE elements studied, there was a statistically significant difference between the groups in the responses to five questions, while the responses to two questions were borderline significant. For twenty-six of the thirty-three questions, the NDE elements occurred in both groups with statistically equal frequency.

The conclusion: All near-death experience elements appearing in Western NDEs are present in non-Western NDEs. There are many non-Western NDEs with narratives that are strikingly similar to the narratives of typical Western NDEs. At a minimum, it may be concluded that non-Western NDEs are much more similar to Western NDEs than dissimilar. Recall that slightly over half of the non-Western near-death experiences studied were shared in languages other than English. Earlier in this chapter we found that language translation issues appear to account for significant differences in the content of NDEs from around the world—differences that probably do not actually exist. With these considerations, I believe a reasonable interpretation of the NDERF study findings are that non-Western NDEs appear to be akin to Western NDEs. If there are any differences at all between non-Western and Western NDEs, the differences are more likely to be minor than substantial.[3]

At NDERF we have not yet received enough English NDEs from non-Western countries to be able to directly compare them with English NDEs from predominantly English-speaking countries. I expect that someday we will have enough English NDEs from non-Western countries to allow such a comparison. That will certainly be an interesting study.

Until now, all NDERF study findings presented in this

book have been consistent with the findings of scores of prior NDE studies. The NDERF study of non-Western NDEs was different, as the findings from this part of the NDERF study are dissimilar from the conclusions of prior studies of non-Western NDEs.

From our prior discussion, it is easy to see how difficult it is to study non-Western near-death experiences. Several researchers have done the best they could with existing data and tried to reach conclusions about non-Western NDEs. These researchers were aware of the difficulties with this type of research, and their conclusions are recognized as tentative.

One of the leading researchers of non-Western NDEs is Dr. Allan Kellehear, a sociology professor. He reviewed previously published reports of non-Western near-death experiences and studied five NDE elements. He concluded that deceased or supernatural beings commonly appeared in non-Western NDEs. He also found that non-Western NDEs commonly described otherworldly visits. Both of these elements are also common in Western NDEs. However, Dr. Kellehear's review found some differences between his study group of non-Western and Western NDEs. He states: "Life review and the tunnel experience seem to be culture-specific features."[4]

Is this so? From the NDERF study of 19 non-Western NDEs and comparison group of 583 NDEs, I looked at the NDERF survey questions regarding life reviews and tunnels.

There were two questions about life review, with some differences in the wording of the questions. In response to the survey question "Did you experience a review of past events in your life?" the two groups answered as follows:

	Western NDEs	Non-Western NDEs
Yes	128	4
Uncertain	49	0
No	406	15

There was no statistically significant difference in the responses between the two groups. The second survey question relating to life review was an NDE Scale question that asked, "Did scenes from your past come back to you?" Responses allowed to this question were "Past flashed before me, out of my control," "Remembered many past events," and "No." A life review was considered to have occurred if either of the first two responses to this question was selected—that is, any option but "No." A life review was present in 32 percent of the non-Western NDE group and 25 percent of the Western NDE group. This was not a statistically significant difference. In view of the responses to both of these questions, the life review appears to be present and occur with equal frequency in both non-Western and Western NDEs.

What about tunnel experiences? There was one NDERF survey question that asked, "Did you pass into or through a tunnel or enclosure?" Responses to this question were:

	Western NDEs	Non-Western NDEs
Yes	188	8
Uncertain	97	1
No	298	10

There was no statistically significant difference in the responses between the two groups. As with life reviews, tunnel experiences appear to occur in both non-Western and Western NDEs, and with equal frequency. The NDERF study found no evidence that life reviews or tunnel experiences are culture-specific features of near-death experiences.

Throughout this book we have found no significant cultural influences on the content of NDEs. This includes the results from our study of very small children, age five and younger, whose NDEs appeared identical to those of older children and adults. We also found no cultural influence whatsoever in the content of NDEs shared in English from predominantly non-English-speaking countries from around the world. Moreover, we have analyzed NDEs occurring under general anesthesia. These NDErs cannot have had any conscious memories at the time of their experience, including memories that are culturally determined.

In researching non-Western NDE accounts from other sources, I have found some that seem to include a life-threatening event at the time of the experience but with content quite different from typical Western near-death experiences. I can't tell if this apparent difference in NDE content is real or due to language translation issues. It is also possible that even if the content of near-death experiences is the same across the different cultures of the world, the NDErs may interpret their experiences differently. To quote leading NDE researcher Dr. Bruce Greyson and associates: "Even the cross-cultural differences observed suggest that it is not the core experience that differs but the ways in which people interpret what they have experienced."[5]

I coauthored a scholarly book chapter that reviewed

thirty years of research about the characteristics of Western NDEs. In this review we were unable to find any characteristics of Western NDEs that could be considered to be culturally determined. We concluded:

> Researchers so far have tended to find that most hypothesized predictors of NDE occurrence, incidence, contents, and aftereffects are not reliable.[6]

At NDERF we have received many dozens of non-Western near-death experiences. Many of these NDEs were shared as narratives only, without the NDErs completing the NDERF questionnaire. From reviewing all of NDERF's non-Western near-death experiences, I find that these non-Western NDEs are generally similar to Western NDEs.[7]

In summary, the NDERF study found the narratives of non-Western NDEs to be generally similar to Western NDEs. Directly comparing the elements of non-Western and Western near-death experiences revealed that all elements that occurred in Western NDEs were found in non-Western NDEs as well. As we saw in our study of NDEs around the world, language translation issues may account for apparent, but not real, differences in the content of non-Western and Western near-death experiences.[8] Any differences that might exist between non-Western and Western NDEs are likely minor.

MORE EVIDENCE FOR THE AFTERLIFE

The NDERF cross-cultural NDE study found near-death experiences to be remarkably similar around the world, including NDEs that take place in Western and non-Western countries. This is further evidence that NDEs are much more than simply a product of cultural beliefs or prior life experiences. Near-death experiences remind us that although the people on earth may be a world apart, they may share this important spiritual experience. It's amazing to think that no matter what country we call home, perhaps our real home is in the wondrous unearthly realms consistently described by NDErs around the world.

PROOF #9: CHANGED LIVES

If men define situations as real, they are
real in their consequences.
—**William Isaac Thomas**

It is difficult for most of us to imagine what it's like to have a near-death experience. To begin with, a person who has had one has nearly died. Nobody expects to *nearly* die, let alone die. As Sigmund Freud put it so succinctly, "When we attempt to imagine death, we perceive ourselves as spectators."

When a near-death experience takes place, it is generally completely different from anything people could have imagined ever happening to them. When NDErs describe their experience as being "unworldly," they are generally understating it. Words like *unworldly* don't begin to explain an experience that takes you out of your physical body and into realms described so vividly in the dozens of NDE accounts we have presented so far.

BARRIERS TO SHARING

It is a long journey from the time a near-death experience takes place until the changes following the experience are fully manifested. These life changes often include transformations in the near-death experiencer's values, beliefs, and relations with others. Collectively, these changes are called *aftereffects*.

Near-death experiencers often tell me that the aftereffects were the most important part of their experiences. As we will see in this chapter, aftereffects can dramatically affect the NDEr for the rest of his or her life. To understand NDE aftereffects, it is helpful to "walk a mile" with NDErs, following what happens from the time of the NDE until the aftereffects become fully manifest later in life.

For NDErs, the first challenge is usually to recover from what nearly killed them. After regaining consciousness following their life-threatening event, NDErs may have to deal with both the shock of their life-threatening event and the memory of their near-death experience.

Many people believe that NDErs would jump at the opportunity to share such a dramatic experience immediately after it happens. In reality, this is not usually the case. After recovering from nearly dying, if they try to share their story, they often encounter another challenge: they may be met with indifference and even negative reactions. It's easy to understand how crushed a near-death experiencer would be, trying to share how remarkable the experience was, only to be told that the NDE was due to drugs, hallucinations, or a dream or was imaginary and never really happened. When NDErs encounter such inappropriate reactions from others, they may suppress their experience and their memory of it.

If they do, the possibility that they will develop life-enhancing aftereffects is greatly reduced.

Compounding the difficulty NDErs face in sharing is that near-death experiences are often so unworldly that they may be difficult to express in words. Near-death experiences are often called "ineffable," not only because they are difficult to explain in words, but also because it may be difficult to mentally process these astounding experiences. People may struggle for a long time to understand what has happened to them, and they may believe that others won't understand either.

Still, some NDErs bravely try to share their experience with medical personnel shortly after it occurs. Sometimes they are lucky enough to find nurses or doctors who understand NDEs and are sympathetic. Unfortunately, this is often not the case. Many in the medical profession are uninformed about NDEs or just plain don't care. The result is a negative response and a look that says, "You must be crazy." Imagine how traumatic it is for NDErs to encounter reactions like this one when they share their experiences.

Daniel, who lives in Peru, nearly died from meningitis. Here's what happened when he tried to share his near-death experience:

I told some people about my experience, and they said I was crazy. My own doctor had me get psychiatric help because I said that I spoke with God.

Near-death experiencers may be very uncomfortable sharing their NDE with their medical caregivers. This was the case with Juanita, who nearly died from a hemorrhage after delivery.

I never told my doctor or nurses. I felt they would think I was crazy!

It's no wonder that medical personnel have a difficult time knowing how to respond to a patient's near-death experience. Most patients at first don't know how to respond to them either. The unexpected nature of an NDE presents a significant barrier to sharing the experience. Most NDErs who share their case study with NDERF did not know what a near-death experience was at the time it occurred. An NDERF survey question asks, "Did you have any knowledge of near-death experience (NDE) prior to your experience?" A resounding 66.4 percent of respondents—nearly two-thirds—answered "No." Only 12.7 percent of NDErs questioned in the NDERF study felt that their experience, when it occurred, included features consistent with their beliefs. Understandably, it would be difficult to talk about such a profound experience, especially if you didn't believe that anything of its kind could take place.

These barriers to sharing NDEs clarify why many NDErs do not speak of their experience for years or even decades. However, the great majority of NDErs—more than 90 percent in the NDERF survey—eventually shared their experiences with other people.

TRANSFORMATIVE CHANGES

While people who have a near-death experience often share it first with their immediate family and spouse, we found in the NDERF study that eventually many do talk about their

NDE freely, including the aftereffects and associated positive changes that have taken place in their lives as a result of the experience. The original version of the NDERF study questionnaire asked, "Has your life changed specifically as a result of your experience?" Of those responding, 73.1 percent answered "Yes," 12.7 percent answered "Uncertain," and only 14.2 percent answered "No." Thus the great majority, but not all, of NDErs experienced changes in their lives as a result of their near-death experience.

The percentage of NDErs selecting "No" in response to this survey question must be interpreted with caution. Some NDErs completed the survey shortly after their near-death experience. They may experience changes later in life as a result of their experience. Other studies have shown that it takes as long as seven years or more for a person who has a near-death experience to fully integrate into their life the changes that resulted from the experience. Near-death-experience researcher P. M. H. Atwater studied this and concluded, "My research has shown that it takes the average child or adult experiencer a minimum of seven years to successfully adjust to what happened to them."[1]

Many different aftereffects of near-death experiences have been described in prior studies. One of the earliest studies found that NDErs described more self-confidence, a stronger sense of spirituality, a reduced interest in material gain or status, and a greater appreciation of life.[2] Later research found a myriad of other aftereffects, including a belief in the sacredness of life, a sense of God's presence, and an awareness of meaning and purpose in life. Near-death experiencers often become increasingly aware of the needs of others and are willing to reach out to them. They may seek to live life more fully and joyfully. Personally speaking, I think the world needs a lot more people with values like these.

Following their near-death experience, many people become more religious or spiritual. They may become increasingly committed to their preexisting religious practices. Other NDErs become less interested in traditional religious practices, especially if their religious group was dismissive or negative about their NDE.

Near-death experiencers usually undergo not just one aftereffect but many. Developing these major changes in values and understandings takes time. It also takes a lot of work. In a real sense, NDErs may feel reborn into their new beliefs and values. Those who manifest substantial changes may seem to have become completely different people to their friends and family. The great majority of NDErs find their aftereffects to be positive and life-enhancing. It is very uncommon for NDErs to have prolonged negative or life-diminishing aftereffects, though this has been reported.

Experiencing a change in values may lead NDErs to reevaluate their jobs. For example, at the time of their near-death experience, they may have been in occupations that valued cutthroat competition and a "win at all costs" mentality. With their values shifting toward compassion and reduced materialistic beliefs, they now find that such occupations increasingly conflict with their new way of looking at the world. No longer sharing the values of their workplaces, they may change occupations. By contrast, if their occupations emphasize positive interpersonal interactions and serving others, their compassionate values may result in their becoming star job performers.

Near-death experiencers may reevaluate their existing interpersonal relationships. They may find the courage to end negative and unloving relationships. Often they seek out positive and loving relationships that are more in line with their new values. Many NDErs find that their increasingly loving and compassionate interaction with others results in stronger marriages and relationships.

The skeptics claim that all these aftereffects following a near-death experience are due to the experience of nearly dying rather than to the NDE itself. Perhaps, they claim, it's the close brush with death, not the NDE, that explains the life changes that take place later. Once again, as we have seen consistently throughout this book, the facts contradict the skeptics' claims.

Two prospective studies of cardiac arrest survivors found that it is mainly the near-death experience and not just the close brush with death that results in the positive life-changing aftereffects.[3] In both studies, all the participants had a cardiac arrest and nearly died. The study participants were divided into two groups: those who had a near-death experience and those who did not. The studies assessed aftereffects in both groups. Both studies found that the NDErs described many more aftereffects than the cardiac arrest survivors who did not have a near-death experience. Both studies found that the aftereffects reported by NDErs increased over time.

Three studies also found that NDEs with more detailed content, often referred to as more "depth" in the NDE, were strongly correlated with the occurrence of more aftereffects.[4] These studies further establish that it is mainly the near-death experience that results in the aftereffects.

The changes experienced by NDErs are usually both profound and lasting. Pim van Lommel, MD, the medical researcher in the Netherlands who has been discussed elsewhere in this book, discovered a lot about the transformations NDErs undergo in his study of cardiac arrest survivors. Here is what he had to say about the transformative effects of NDEs:

> [My work] was designed to assess whether the transformation in attitude toward life and death following an NDE is the result of having an NDE or the result of the cardiac arrest itself. In this follow-up research into transformational processes after NDE, we found a significant difference between patients with and without an NDE. The process of transformation took several years to consolidate. Patients with an NDE did not show any fear of death, they strongly believed in an afterlife, and their insight in what is important in life had changed: love and compassion for oneself, for others, and for nature. They now understood the cosmic law that everything one does to others will ultimately be returned to oneself: hatred and violence as well as love and compassion. Remarkably, there was often evidence of increased intuitive feelings. Furthermore, the long-lasting transformational effects of an experience that lasts only a few minutes was a surprising and unexpected finding.[5]

Let's take a closer look at some of the more common and interesting NDE aftereffects.

Increased Value of Loving Interactions

Love is one of the most common words NDErs use to describe their experience, and for good reason. People who have a near-death experience often become more loving in their interactions with others and increasingly value positive and empathic relations. Occasionally the NDErs' desire to relate compassionately to others leads them to change jobs and enter the healing professions. When asked in the NDERF study questionnaire, "Have your relationships changed specifically as a result of your experience?," 57.3 percent answered "Yes," and many went on to elaborate.

Jewel, who nearly drowned while bodysurfing, wrote,

Certainly it is in the best interests of yourself and everyone you meet to be the most kind and courteous that you can be. Treat everyone as you would like to be treated. We meet simply another version of ourselves every day.

Rusty, who nearly died from loss of blood, wrote,

My outlook on life and what I hold to be important has changed. My experiences and interactions with other people, especially my family, have gained importance.

Donna, who was nearly strangled to death, reported,

I was withdrawn and victimized before. I attracted bad people and didn't see it. I still seem to attract some bad ones, but I see it. I am very independent, strong, focused, but can be too loving and too giving. I have fewer and need fewer relationships, but those I have are more meaningful.

Gwen, whose heart stopped from pneumonia, wrote,

I never was patient before; now I have lots and lots of patience. I have a lot of discernment too, which I didn't have before. I have empathy and understand that none of us are ever going to be perfect in this life.

Although NDErs tend to become more compassionate and loving, the NDERF study shows that the changes experienced by NDErs may not be well received by those around them. Friends and family members may find it difficult to relate to changes in values and interests that take place as a result of a near-death experience. Also, NDErs may be less willing to tolerate relationships that are unloving. One NDEr named Joyce summed it up succinctly:

I think it planted a seed that helped me choose better partners for myself and never to be in another abusive relationship.

Overall, though, NDErs tend to become increasingly loving and accepting of *themselves*. This is especially noticeable if their NDE resulted from a suicide attempt, in which case the NDEr will rarely attempt suicide again.[6]

A study from 1975, before near-death experiences were well known, presented the results of interviews with seven of only ten known survivors of jumping off the Golden Gate Bridge. All seven of these suicide attempters described after-effects of spiritual rebirth and transformed lives. As one jumper said, "It affirmed my belief—there is a higher spiritual world. I experienced a transcendence—in that moment I was refilled with new hope and purpose of being alive."[7]

On rare occasions I receive e-mails from people, often in the midst of depression, wondering if they should try suicide as a way to induce a near-death experience. My response is an immediate "absolutely no." I encourage those who are depressed to seek counseling and also to discuss their life issues with their health-care team. People who had near-death experiences as a result of suicide attempts almost uniformly believe that their suicide attempts were a serious mistake. A personal experience of NDE should *never* be sought by creating a life-threatening event.

HEALING POWER OF NDEs

As a physician, I am fascinated by NDE accounts suggesting unexpected healings. These inexplicable healings are uncommon but nevertheless deserve mention. I cannot claim with certainty that inexplicable healings occur after NDEs, but the case reports we have suggest this might be happening. One thing I can be certain of from my research is that the possibility of inexplicable healings deserves more attention in NDE research than it has received in the past.

Anita is from Hong Kong and was dying from stage 4 Hodgkin's lymphoma. To say she was dying is no exaggeration: the senior cancer doctor gave her thirty-six hours to live. Anita became unconscious. She had an out-of-body experience and was able to see her doctor talking to her husband about forty feet down the hall outside her room. She later verified her OBE observations with her husband, who was "shocked." The healing associated with her near-death experience is among the most dramatic ever reported. Anita tells what happened:

I was made to understand that, as tests had been taken for my organ functions (and the results were not out yet), that if I chose life, the results would show that my organs were functioning normally. If I chose death, the results would show organ failure as the cause of death, due to cancer. I was able to change the outcome of the tests by my choice!

I made my choice, and as I started to wake up (in a very confused state, as I could not at that time tell which side of the veil I was on), the doctors came rushing into the room with big smiles on their faces, saying to my family, "Good news—we got the results, and her organs are functioning—we can't believe it! Her body really did seem like it had shut down!"

After that, I began to recover rapidly. The doctors had been waiting for me to become stable before doing a lymph node biopsy to track the type of cancer cells, and they could not even find a lymph node big enough to suggest cancer. (Upon entering the hospital my body was filled with swollen lymph nodes.) They did a bone marrow biopsy, again to find the cancer activity so they could adjust the chemotherapy according to the disease, and there wasn't any in the bone marrow. The doctors were very confused but put it down to me suddenly responding to the chemo. Because they themselves were unable to understand what was going on, they made me undergo test after test, all of which I passed with flying colors, and clearing every test empowered me even more! I had a full body scan, and because they could not find anything, they made the radiologist repeat it again!"

Because of my experience, I am now sharing with everyone I know that miracles are possible in your life every day. After what I have seen, I realize that absolutely anything is possible, and that we did not come here to suffer. Life is supposed to be great, and we are very, very loved. The way I look at life has changed dramatically, and I am so glad to have been given a second chance to experience "heaven on earth."

One case report of incredible healing after a near-death experience came from Geralyn. At the age of thirteen, Geralyn was fighting for her life. She had the most advanced stage of a highly aggressive malignancy called Burkitt's lymphoma. Both her near-death experience and her healing were dramatic:

It was three months into being diagnosed with Burkitt's lymphoma. At the time, due to my age (thirteen), I was not told of the severity of the illness. Only my parents and elders in my family knew that I was given a 1 percent chance of survival. In fact, the doctors told them that they should prepare for my "arrangements" as they believed I was not going to survive this illness. The disease had ravished my body, and the spleen, liver, and intestines were filled with tumors.

One evening, while hospitalized, I was eating some popcorn when suddenly I began to feel this immense pain in my stomach. I felt the need to pass my bowels but could not. Two days later I still could not and began regurgitating my food. It was discovered that a large tumor was blocking my bowels. I was immediately sent to surgery.

During the surgery I died. For how long, I cannot say, but I had no sensation of passing. I went from lying on the gurney to floating in the air above the doctors. I watched as they pulled out my intestines, carefully laying them to the side of my body, and then they began racing around (I presume in an attempt to revive me). During this, I began rising, and all at once it seemed as though I knew everything there was to know. It seemed as if all the mysteries of the world were being revealed. I understood science, math, life! Simultaneously, I could see people below me in other rooms; I saw my grandmother and great-aunt crying outside the operating area. I saw other patients being treated in other surgery rooms. I saw people outside the hospital. I saw so much, and I continued to rise.

Then as instantly as I rose, I was instantly present within something that resembled a cloud. I don't say it was a cloud, but it was bright, white, and soft. I felt the total embrace of love. And I knew I was in a place of great safety and warmth. I saw what could have been angels, three. They had great peace about them, and they were part of this "cloud," as if attached directly to it. They didn't say anything to me, yet I felt the grandness of them and their joy. I was happy, peaceful, and desired to stay amongst them.

Suddenly a large hand came towards me. I can't even express its size as everything there was more than words could express. All I know is that it was a nonthreatening hand, and it glowed with an overpowering light. Then I heard a voice that seemed soft yet authoritative tell me, "My child, go back, for you have much work left to do!" I was instantly back in my body. Instantly! When I awoke, I told the doctors what I saw them doing to me during the operation. They were amazed at my precise [description] of their work. Actually, they had removed two and a half feet of my intestines. Still, they didn't believe the story. I also remember feeling angry that I had to return. I knew that I was healed. The doctors were awestruck to find that after only one chemo treatment the tumors were gone. And that treatment was given against my will as I was too young for them to hear my protest. And thirty-seven years later, I am still here.

Another story of unexplained healing came from a man named Denver who lived in Florida. Denver was in the hospital with blood clots in his lungs, a very dangerous condition that often leads to death. As Denver struggled to breathe, the doctor made the decision to give him high doses of blood thinner.

Although the blood thinner began to treat the clots, another equally serious problem arose. Denver's stomach and other organs began to hemorrhage due to the large dose of blood thinner.

Denver's mother was told that the young man had only a 15 percent chance of surviving. During the night while hovering close to death, Denver had a near-death experience. In this NDE he was asked if he was "prepared to leave." He declined, and continued to cling to life. The doctor decided to move him to a larger regional hospital, where his chances of survival were greater.

Denver was rushed to the regional hospital. He tells the rest of the story:

When I arrived forty-five minutes later at the regional hospital, and the expert began running X-rays and other tests, he called the doctor in Niceville very frustrated. The [Niceville] doctor quoted him as saying, "Doctor, you send me a dying boy needing surgery, and I'll be damned if I can find a thing wrong with him!" The doctor was floored! Later during my follow-up visits to see the doctor after being released from ICU, the doctor kept repeating that he saw no other alternative but to call this a miracle from God!

Many such examples of apparent unexplained healings associated with near-death experiences have been shared with NDERF. Time and again the people who write these case studies use words like *miracle* or *I was healed*.

One of the best documented examples of healing following a near-death experience was reported by Dr. Penny Sartori and associates.[8] The NDE she described was part of a prospective study of near-death experiences. This case report was remarkable both for the accurate out-of-body observations during the NDE and also for the inexplicable healing following the NDE.

The patient in this case report had emergency surgery for bowel cancer. As he was recovering from surgery, his clinical condition worsened and he became comatose. While deeply unconscious, and with his eyes closed, he had a near-death experience. His NDE included an out-of-body experience with detailed observations of events going on around his body. After his recovery he described what he saw happening around him while he was unconscious. His OBE observations were confirmed as accurate by those caring for him during his near-death experience.

This near-death experiencer had been born with cerebral palsy. As a result, he had a contracted and deformed hand, which throughout his life he had not been able to open completely. After his NDE he was able to open and use his hand for the first time in his life. This medically inexplicable healing was corroborated by his family and health-care team.

I don't know how these healings take place or even if they take place as a result of the NDEs. I do know, however, that a significant number of NDErs express a belief that they were healed during their NDE, which is reason for further research. Exploring these seemingly miraculous healings further will be a direction I take in the future.

Psychic Changes

There are many people who have a hard time accepting anything labeled "psychic." I can understand this, as I felt that way before I started my research into near-death experiences. However, as I read more about NDEs I became aware of dozens of scholarly articles that described psychic NDE aftereffects.[9]

People who have near-death experiences often believe they have increased psychic abilities following their experience. These are not people who gaze into crystal balls or dress like gypsies. Rather, they are people who are ordinary to the core but with one great difference: their ordinary life has been touched by an extraordinary NDE. Following their NDEs, many describe such psychic abilities as empathy (the ability to tell how another person feels), intuition, or precognitive skills.

In the NDERF study, 45.0 percent of those surveyed answered "Yes" to the question "Did you have any psychic, paranormal, or other special gifts following the experience you did not have prior to the experience?" Of the remaining, 19.1 percent weren't sure, and 35.9 percent answered "No." Although a positive response of 45 percent is astounding, I think the actual number might be higher. Those NDErs who were small children at the time of the experience may not know if their current psychic gifts were present before the NDE. Also, some NDErs describe dramatically heightened psychic abilities immediately after their experiences that diminish in a variable amount of time.

Here are but a few of the many stories we have collected at NDERF. These examples will give you an idea of some of the psychic abilities described by NDErs.

Romona was in an aluminum boat that slammed into a

barge and flipped over. Romona was trapped beneath the barge. Struggling to reach the surface, she ran out of air and felt herself leave her body. She said that she felt "fine and so happy" in this out-of-body state.

Rescued and resuscitated with CPR, Romona discovered that she had psychic aftereffects. One of her best examples came on the telephone with her sister. Romona tells the story:

My brother-in-law, [Bob], died in 2000. He did not believe in the afterlife. I was on the phone with my sister, [Marsha], who lived in Walnut Creek, California. All at once I only could see yellow, like someone put a yellow sheet of paper in front of my eyes. Then it was gone, and then my den appeared to be filled with bubbles, thousands of bubbles. This kept happening—the color yellow then gone, thousands of bubbles then gone. Then I had a voice in my head saying, "Tell her, tell her, tell her." It became so loud I couldn't even hear my sister anymore. I then said, "Marsha, I have to tell you something. It makes no sense, I am not crazy, but I have to tell you: yellow bubbles." She couldn't believe it. She was happy, so happy. She then told me one night that she and . . . Bob watched a movie called Houdini. *Bob was making a comment of there being no afterlife. Marsha told him she would think of a secret word . . . and whoever went first—if there was an afterlife—to somehow get the secret word to the one left here. To my surprise those were the secret words:* yellow bubbles. *She picked them because it made no sense; nobody would ever just blurt out those words.*

Marcia was under a one-and-a-half-ton structure when it collapsed. Marcia had an out-of-body experience, and then her late father and sister appeared to her. Her sister had died of brain cancer several years earlier and her father had died about four months earlier. Her father kept telling her to breathe.

Marcia survived. After her NDE Marcia had premonitions about future events. This is one of the more striking:

I woke one morning and told my husband that a friend and business associate of my husband's had died. I had talked to this man on the phone at some point over a fifteen-year period, but I [had] never met him. He wasn't someone that I thought about. I just matter-of-factly told my husband that he died. A short time later my husband got a phone call, and a friend told him that this man had died. . . . When my husband got the phone call and the man told him who had died, my husband remarked that he already knew about it. Then my husband remembered that it was I who had told him. I have had other premonitions about events that were to happen, but they weren't life-shattering things. I just knew different things that were to happen prior to them actually happening.

I love the casual way in which NDErs tell these psychic events. As one NDEr told my coauthor, "I have come to realize that we all have the ability to 'read' one another. There is just something about the near-death experience that triggers that ability in us."[10]

Although there has been a substantial amount of research into psychic near-death-experience aftereffects, few researchers have directly tested the psychic abilities of NDErs. This will certainly be an important area for future NDE research.

If I have discovered anything by starting NDERF, it's that near-death experiences touch on a lifetime of questions that, to answer one, leads to a dozen more.

Decreased Fear of Death

Few of us experience mortality as directly as do people who
have had near-death experiences. Yet despite having the fright-
ful experience of nearly dying, most NDErs do not report an
increase in their fear of death, but rather a decrease in their
fear or a loss of the fear altogether. This is a consistent finding
in a number of previously published studies.[11] Here, in brief, is
what NDErs have to say about death:

Catherine, who nearly died after surgery, reported,

*I had always been terrified of death, of oblivion. I no longer fear
death.*

Lauren was felt by the EMS to be dead on arrival after a
severe accident. She wrote,

*I am no longer afraid of death. I know now in my soul that there
is so much more after life. I feel that once I have learned what it
is I am supposed to learn or a task that I must complete, that I
will be rewarded with a life after death!*

Sharla, who nearly died of respiratory arrest, wrote,

*The most significant part of the experience is that there is (to
me) nothing to fear of death.*

The fear of death is one of humanity's most powerful
sources of anxiety. There are many people today who are so
fearful of death that they are unable to fully live their lives.
For these people, this fear may extend beyond the fear of
their own death; they may fret endlessly about the life and
health of others. The message NDErs share, including their

consistent description of reduced or absent fear of death, is so powerful that I am not surprised when people tell me that their personal fear of death was diminished just by reading accounts of near-death experiences.

Those who have a near-death experience may still fear the actual process of dying. Dying often involves discomfort, though modern medicine has made tremendous progress in easing that discomfort. Dying also involves a separation from our loved ones and all that is familiar in the world. However, the great majority of NDErs believe they experienced first-hand what lies beyond death. And what they experienced beyond death's door leaves many of them fearless when they think about death. For most NDErs, their lack of fear of death is associated with a conviction that death is not final and that a wonderful afterlife is real.

In its own way, the near-death experience has a healing effect on most of the people who have it. People who have a near-death experience may never fear death again. Although they don't necessarily become more religious, NDErs often state that they become more spiritual, and with that change comes a belief in the sacredness of life and a special knowledge that serves to guide them the rest of their lives.

Increased Belief in an Afterlife

People who have a near-death experience are generally convinced that after bodily death a wonderful afterlife awaits them. They believe they personally experienced the afterlife, and they are convinced of its reality. At the NDERF website, people who had a near-death experience have been quite open in describing the afterlife they encountered. We have hundreds of descriptions of what many NDErs describe as "heavenly realms." When these are read consecutively, they provide an impressionistic view of what the heaven of NDEs looks like. Here are a few examples to illustrate what I mean.

David, who had a near-death experience after passing out in the hospital, wrote,

The prairie or meadow in which I found myself walking, the feeling of happiness [that] every blade of grass gave off, that was definitely beautiful, special, and extraordinary.

Robin, who had a near-death experience during a heart attack, reported,

Flatlined—went to a place that was beautifully lit—like the sunshine but much prettier and more golden (kind of like sepia tones). Seemed like a neighborhood, and I was shown around to all the people I loved and missed, and they were all so happy.

Kristin, after a seizure that stopped her heart and breathing, reported,

I feel so tacky saying this since it's so stereotypical, but there was always a bright white light, and I'd go to it, and once I got there, and I touched it, everything was beautifully white and scintillating and warm; it smelled sweet and inviting, like cupcakes or warm vanilla sugar. There were these . . . "unearthly beings," and they talked to me.

Ruben, whose near-death experience took place during cardiac arrest, reported,

At first I was floating, surrounded by a very white and brilliant light, and as I descended I noticed that the white light was not just light: there were very, very white clouds [that] I was passing through. After coming through the clouds I found myself descending toward a very beautiful landscape, with green meadows, rivers, butterflies, and birds. I was moving toward a hill with a tree on top. The sensation I felt I cannot express in words, but it was so wonderfully tranquilizing that the desire is there to return and feel it over again.

It is the experiencing of this kind of heavenly reality that contributes to the NDErs' belief in the afterlife and to their reduced fear of death—and, for that matter, their reduced fear of life. When NDErs have finally processed their experience enough to talk about it, they may share their experience to help others who are grieving, feel hopeless, or doubt an afterlife. Here are some touching and inspiring accounts from NDErs who reached out to others in order to share their conviction that the afterlife does indeed exist, and the profound consolation this brought to others whose loved ones had died.

Mark experienced sudden cardiac death and had a full-blown NDE in which he left his body and went to a heavenly realm. When he returned to life, Mark was blessed with enough psychic abilities to be able to "read" some people. One of the first to experience his newly acquired abilities was a nurse at the office of his cardiologist:

I saw a nurse practitioner in August about three months after. She had all my records and said to me, "You sure had some experience!" I could tell she was in a hurting way, so after she examined me, I shared with her what I saw and felt. She told me what I had just told her was reassuring since she had lost her father less than a year before. She thanked me for sharing it with her and I left. I saw her again two months later. She had turned from a very mousy, timid person [in]to a [person with a] well-dressed, confident look. Not cocky! Self-confident, a broad smile on her face, a cheery attitude. She wanted so to help me with my problems, did so, and as I was leaving the doctor's office she looked into my eyes, past them to my soul, and said simply, "Thank you." That is one of the reasons I believe I was sent back.

Anne nearly died after hemorrhaging blood a few days after childbirth. Her experience, which involved drifting up a tunnel and moving toward a light, was something she kept pretty much to herself. Then she got word that her father was dying and went to visit him in Florida. Realizing she would not see him again, Anne told him of her experience.

The day I left to go home to my family I sat on his bed, and as we said good-bye, both knowing it would be the last time we would see each other, I told him of my experience in order to ease his transition. He thanked me profusely and said that it helped take away the fear.

Belief in an afterlife is one of the most common NDE aftereffects. It's easy to understand why NDErs generally believe there is an afterlife. They believe they've been there. They may have experienced realms that are magnificent beyond anything on earth. And all the other NDE elements, including the out-of-body experience, encountering mystical light, reviewing one's life, and reuniting with deceased loved ones, point to a continuing existence in joy and beauty that transcends physical death.

Near-death experiencers are virtually unanimous that the afterlife is for all of us, not just for those who have had NDEs. This is certainly consistent with their uniform description of the afterlife as a loving and inclusive realm, a realm for us all.

For decades NDEs have been a message of hope to millions of people that there is an afterlife for both themselves and their loved ones. With the latest scientific NDE research, including the new findings from the NDERF study, this message of hope about the afterlife is becoming a promise.

A PIECE OF THE AFTERLIFE

The NDERF study has revealed a lot about the aftereffects of near-death experiences. It has shown the resilience of the human spirit in that facing death is not the end but the beginning. Near-death experiences usually lead to a richer, more fulfilling life. They are transformative in a myriad of ways, inspiring love, creating empathy, and connecting those who experience them more deeply to others. As a near-death experiencer named Colin said, "I have been able to develop deep and fulfilling friendships. I feel the need for friendship much more than I did before the experience. I am able to be a better friend."

The fact that near-death experiences bring about transformation is powerful evidence of the afterlife. For me it's evidence that those who step briefly into the afterlife bring back a piece of it when they return.

Conclusion

After considering the strength of the evidence, I am absolutely convinced that an afterlife exists. I encourage each reader to consider the evidence and come to your own conclusion. A tool to help you determine how convincing you believe the NDE evidence is for an afterlife may be found on the NDERF website at our page exploring evidence of the afterlife (http://www.nderf.org/afterlife).

Nine lines of evidence for the existence of an afterlife have been presented. This evidence would be extraordinary even if NDErs were fully awake and alert at the time of their experiences. But they're not. People who have near-death experiences are generally unconscious or clinically dead at the time of their experience. It is medically inexplicable that they would have *any* conscious experiences, let alone experiences so packed with evidence pointing to an afterlife. To review, these are the nine lines of evidence:

1. The level of consciousness and alertness during near-death experiences is usually *greater* than that experienced during everyday life, even though NDEs generally occur while a person is unconscious or clinically dead. The elements in NDEs generally follow a consistent and logical order.

2. What NDErs see and hear in the out-of-body state during their near-death experiences is generally realistic and often verified later by the NDEr or others as real.

3. Normal or supernormal vision occurs in near-death experiences among those with significantly impaired vision or even legal blindness. Several NDErs who were blind from birth have reported highly visual near-death experiences.

4. Typical near-death experiences occur under general anesthesia at a time when conscious experience should be impossible.

5. Life reviews in near-death experiences include real events that took place in the NDErs' lives, even if the events were forgotten.

6. When NDErs encounter beings they knew from their earthly life, they are virtually always deceased, usually deceased relatives.

7. The near-death experiences of children, including very young children, are strikingly similar to those of older children and adults.

8. Near-death experiences are remarkably consistent around the world. NDEs from non-Western countries appear similar to typical Western NDEs.

9. It is common for NDErs to experience changes in their lives as aftereffects following NDEs. Aftereffects are often powerful and lasting, and the changes follow a consistent pattern.

The NDERF study is the largest scientific study of near-death experience ever reported, and it provides exceptional new scientific evidence for the reality of NDEs and their consistent message of an afterlife. Any one of these nine lines of evidence individually is significant evidence for the reality of near-death experiences and the afterlife. The combination of these nine lines of evidence is so convincing that I believe it is reasonable to accept the existence of an afterlife. I certainly do.

I'm not alone in concluding that near-death experiences are evidence of the afterlife. It's easy to see why those who have a near-death experience accept the reality of their NDE and generally accept the existence of an afterlife. It makes sense that important information about what happens when we die would come from those who actually did nearly die.

The most important findings of the NDERF study have been corroborated by scores of prior scholarly NDE studies over more than thirty years. This certainly helps validate the remarkable NDERF study findings.

This research has profound implications for science. The findings of the NDERF and other NDE studies are consistent with the conclusion that there is far more to consciousness and memory than can be explained solely by our physical brain. I find that incredibly exciting.

We still have much to learn from the scientific study of near-death experiences. Further scientific research of NDEs with a variety of methodologies is encouraged, and NDERF will help in any way we can. Anyone who has had a near-death experience is encouraged to share their account with NDERF no matter what the content of the NDE was.

The arguments of skeptics have consistently failed to explain how near-death experiences occur and why their content is so consistent. There is no earthly experience that consistently reproduces any part of the near-death experience.

There are many who accept the reality of NDEs and want to look deeper into their meaning. At NDERF we are already studying this. Our preliminary findings indicate that there is much more to be learned from NDEs. We are also investigating events other than near-death experiences that suggest an afterlife and may be scientifically studied. Updates on the ongoing NDERF research and additional material related to this book can be found at the NDERF website (http://www.nderf.org/evidence).

This book has important implications for religion. The great religions have always spoken to the belief in God and an afterlife. The evidence of near-death experiences points to an afterlife and a universe guided by a vastly loving intelligence. Near-death experiences consistently reveal that death is not an end but rather a transition to an afterlife. This is a profoundly inspiring thought for us all and for our loved ones. I hope that this book helps to promote such an encouraging message.

For me personally, I'm showing more love to others now than before I started my near-death-experience studies. My understanding of near-death experiences has made me a better doctor. I face life with more courage and confidence. I believe NDErs really do bring back a piece of the afterlife. When NDErs share their remarkable experiences, I believe a piece of the afterlife, in some mysterious way, becomes available to us all.

Notes

Further details about updated research findings, a bibliography, frequently asked questions, errata, NDERF study methodology, and a variety of other topics related to the material presented in this book are available on the NDERF website (http://www.nderf.org/evidence).

The following is not intended to be a comprehensive listing of all references relevant to each chapter. The bibliography available from a link at http://www.nderf.org/evidence will provide an updated listing of the major sources of information about near-death experience and related topics.

Introduction

1. If each of two lines of evidence from near-death experiences (NDEs) is 90 percent convincing of the existence of an afterlife, then the combination of these two lines of evidence may be considered as follows: The probability that either of these lines of NDE evidence *individually* is *not* convincing of the existence of an afterlife is 10 percent, or 0.1. The probability that the *combination* of these two lines of NDE evidence is *not* convincing of the existence of an afterlife is (0.1 x 0.1), or 0.01, which is 1 percent. Thus the *combination* of two lines of NDE evidence, each of which is 90 percent convincing of the existence of an afterlife, gives 100 percent minus 1 percent, or 99 percent confidence that the afterlife is convincingly felt to exist.

2. Raymond Moody, *Life After Life* (Atlanta: Mockingbird Books, 1975).

3. To expand on the inclusion criteria for the 613 NDErs quoted throughout the book: The experience had to describe a single NDE and be

shared in English on the English version of the NDERF survey. Second-person NDE accounts were excluded. These 613 consecutive NDEs that met all criteria were shared between October 2004 and December 2008. Further details regarding the survey methodology can be found at http://www.nderf.org/evidence.

4. The current version of the NDERF survey asks all questions that comprise the NDE Scale. The NDE Scale is described in detail by B. Greyson, "The Near-Death Experience Scale: Construction, Reliability, and Validity," *Journal of Nervous and Mental Disease* 171 (1983): 369–75.

5. There is some variability in what NDE researchers consider the elements of a near-death experience to be. The twelve elements presented here were consistently observed in the NDERF study.

6. Four other major studies used the NDE Scale to study the frequency of NDE elements: B. Greyson, "The Near-Death Experience Scale"; B. Greyson, "Incidence and Correlates of Near-Death Experiences in a Cardiac Care Unit," *General Hospital Psychiatry* 25 (2003): 269–76; A. Pacciolla, "The Near-Death Experience: A Study of Its Validity," *Journal of Near-Death Studies* 14 (1996): 179–85; J. Schwaninger, P. R. Eisenberg, K. B. Schechtman, and A. N. Weiss, "A Prospective Analysis of Near-Death Experiences in Cardiac Arrest Patients," *Journal of Near-Death Studies* 20 (2002): 215–32. The preceding four studies had a combined total of 136 NDErs.

7. A discussion of frightening NDEs is beyond the scope of this book. Those interested in this topic are encouraged to read the presentation of frightening NDEs at the link on the NDERF website at http://www.nderf.org/evidence.

8. Pew Forum on Religion and Public Life, U.S. Religious Landscape Survey, Summary of Key Findings, http://religions.pewforum.org/pdf/report2religious-landscape-study-key-findings.pdf.

Chapter 1: First Encounters

1. R. Blacher, "To Sleep, Perchance to Dream . . . ," *Journal of the American Medical Association* 242, no. 21 (1979): 2291.

2. M. Sabom, "The Near-Death Experience," *Journal of the American Medical Association* 244, no. 1 (1980): 29–30.

3. R. Moody, *Life After Life* (Atlanta: Mockingbird Books, 1975).

4. R. Moody, *Reflections on Life After Life* (New York: Stackpole Books, 1977), 113.

5. R. Moody and P. Perry, *Coming Back: A Psychiatrist Explores Past-Life Journeys* (New York: Bantam, 1991), 11.

6. R. Moody and P. Perry, *The Light Beyond* (New York: Bantam Books, 1988), 62.

7. The discussion between Sheila (not her real name) and me took place over a quarter of a century ago. I cannot recall the exact details of this discussion. Sheila's NDE is presented as accurately as I can remember it. I cannot be as confident of the details of Sheila's NDE as I am of the other NDEs presented in this book from written accounts shared directly by NDErs with NDERF.

Chapter 2: Journey Toward Understanding

1. B. Eadie, *Embraced by the Light* (New York: Bantam, 1992).

2. G. Gallup Jr. and W. Proctor, *Adventures in Immortality: A Look Beyond the Threshold of Death* (New York: McGraw-Hill, 1982). There is significant uncertainty regarding the prevalence of NDEs, but this study's estimate of 5 percent is widely quoted in spite of its methodological issues.

3. A number of published studies directly compared the reliability of Internet surveys with "pencil-and-paper" surveys. The general consensus of multiple studies suggests that Internet surveys are as reliable as "pencil-and-paper" surveys. A detailed discussion of this topic is found through a link on the page http://www.nderf.org/evidence.

4. D. Karnofsky and J. Burchenal, "The Clinical Evaluation of Chemotherapeutic Agents in Cancer," in *Evaluation of Chemotherapeutic Agents,* ed. C. M. MacLeod (New York: Columbia University Press, 1949), 191–205.

5. NDErs sharing with NDERF may request that their NDEs not be posted on the NDERF website. Less than 5 percent of the NDErs request this. This helps assure that the near-death-experience accounts posted on the NDERF website are fully representative of all near-death experiences shared with NDERF. A detailed discussion of how representative the

NDEs shared with NDERF are of all NDEs is at a link on the page http://www.nderf.org/evidence.

6. A few of the NDEs that needed to be presented in this book were cases in which we could not contact the NDErs. When these NDEs are presented they are paraphrased, for ethical reasons. All paraphrased NDEs in this book are introduced as paraphrased accounts. All paraphrased NDEs are posted on the NDERF website in their original form.

Chapter 3: Proof #1: Lucid Death

1. Following a cardiac arrest, EEG changes consistent with decreased blood flow to the brain are seen in about six seconds. The EEG flatlines in ten to twenty seconds. See J. W. DeVries, P. F. A. Bakker, G. H. Visser, J. C. Diephuis, and A. C. van Huffelen, "Changes in Cerebral Oxygen Uptake and Cerebral Electrical Activity During Defibrillation Threshold Testing," *Anesthesiology and Analgesia* 87 (1998): 16–20.

2. Near-death experiences associated with cardiac arrest have been reported in dozens of previously published studies. Over one hundred NDEs occurring during cardiac arrest have been reported in these five studies alone: M. Sabom, *Recollections of Death: A Medical Investigation* (New York: Simon & Schuster, 1982); P. van Lommel, R. van Wees, V. Meyers, and I. Elfferich, "Near-Death Experience in Survivors of Cardiac Arrest: A Prospective Study in the Netherlands," *Lancet* 358 (2001): 2039–45; S. Parnia, D. G. Waller, R. Yeates, and P. Fenwick, "A Qualitative and Quantitative Study of the Incidence, Features and Aetiology of Near Death Experiences in Cardiac Arrest Survivors," *Resuscitation* 48 (2001): 149–56; J. Schwaninger, P. R. Eisenberg, K. B. Schechtman, and A. N. Weiss, "A Prospective Analysis of Near-Death Experiences in Cardiac Arrest Patients," *Journal of Near-Death Studies* 20 (2002): 215–32; B. Greyson, "Incidence and Correlates of Near-Death Experiences in a Cardiac Care Unit," *General Hospital Psychiatry* 25 (2003): 269–76.

3. B. Greyson, E. W. Kelly, and E. F. Kelly, "Explanatory Models for Near-Death Experiences," in *The Handbook of Near-Death Experiences: Thirty Years of Investigation,* ed. J. Holden, B. Greyson, and D. James (Westport, CT: Praeger Publishers, 2009), 229.

4. Prior NDE studies consistently describe enhanced mental functioning during the experience. Here are two illustrative studies: J. E. Owens, E. W. Cook, and I. Stevenson, "Features of 'Near-Death Experience' in Relation to Whether or Not Patients Were Near Death," *Lancet* 336 (1990): 1175–77; E. W. Kelly, B. Greyson, and E. F. Kelly, "Unusual Experiences Near Death and Related Phenomena," in *Irreducible Mind: Toward a Psychology for the 21st Century,* by E. F. Kelly, E. W. Kelly, A. Crabtree, A. Gauld, M. Grosso, and B. Greyson (Lanham, MD: Rowman & Littlefield, 2007), 367–421, quote on 386.

5. J. Long and J. Long, "A Comparison of NDEs Occurring Before and After 1975: Results from a Web Survey of Near Death Experiencers," *Journal of Near-Death Studies* 22, no. 1 (2003): 21–32.

6. G. K. Athappilly, B. Greyson, and I. Stevenson, "Do Prevailing Societal Models Influence Reports of Near-Death Experiences? A Comparison of Accounts Reported Before and After 1975," *Journal of Nervous and Mental Disease* 194 (2006): 218.

Chapter 4: Proof #2: Out of Body

1. M. Sabom, *Recollections of Death: A Medical Investigation* (New York: Simon & Schuster, 1982).

2. P. Sartori, "A Prospective Study of NDEs in an Intensive Therapy Unit," *Christian Parapsychologist* 16, no. 2 (2004): 34–40. Results of this study were later presented in further detail: P. Sartori, *The Near-Death Experiences of Hospitalized Intensive Care Patients: A Five Year Clinical Study* (Lewiston, NY: Edwin Mellen Press, 2008).

3. J. Holden, "Veridical Perception in Near-Death Experiences," in *The Handbook of Near-Death Experiences: Thirty Years of Investigation*, ed. J. Holden, B. Greyson, and D. James (Westport, CT: Praeger Publishers, 2009).

4. K. Clark, "Clinical Interventions with Near-Death Experiencers," in *The Near-Death Experience: Problems, Prospects, Perspectives,* ed. B. Greyson and C. P. Flynn (Springfield, IL: Charles C. Thomas, 1984), 242–55.

5. K. Augustine, "Does Paranormal Perception Occur in Near-Death Experiences?" *Journal of Near-Death Studies* 25, no. 4 (2007): 203–36; Sharp, K. C. "The Other Shoe Drops: Commentary on 'Does Paranormal

Perception Occur in Near-Death Experiences?'" *Journal of Near-Death Studies* 25, no. 4 (2007): 245–50.

6. P. van Lommel, R. van Wees, V. Meyers, and I. Elfferich, "Near-Death Experience in Survivors of Cardiac Arrest: A Prospective Study in the Netherlands," *Lancet* 358 (2001): 2039–45.

7. For more information on the AWARE study, see University of Southampton Media Centre, "World's Largest Ever Study of Near-Death Experiences," http://www.soton.ac.uk/mediacentre/news/2008/sep/08_165.shtml.

8. People experiencing cardiac arrest are usually amnesic or confused regarding events occurring immediately prior to or after the cardiac arrest. Here are three illustrative studies: M. J. Aminoff, M. M. Scheinman, J. C. Griffin, and J. M. Herre, "Electrocerebral Accompaniments of Syncope Associated with Malignant Ventricular Arrhythmias," *Annals of Internal Medicine* 108 (1988): 791–96; P. van Lommel, R. van Wees, V. Meyers, and I. Elfferich, "Near-Death Experience in Survivors of Cardiac Arrest: A Prospective Study in the Netherlands," *Lancet* 358 (2001): 2039–45; S. Parnia and P. Fenwick, "Near Death Experiences in Cardiac Arrest: Visions of a Dying Brain or Visions of a New Science of Consciousness," *Resuscitation* 52, no. 1 (2002): 5–11.

9. There have been multiple reports from other NDE researchers of NDErs observing earthly events far from their physical bodies and beyond any possible physical sensory awareness. Here are two studies containing fifteen NDEs with corroboration of the NDErs' remote observations by others: E. W. Cook, B. Greyson, and I. Stevenson, "Do Any Near-Death Experiences Provide Evidence for the Survival of Human Personality After Death? Relevant Features and Illustrative Case Reports," *Journal of Scientific Exploration* 12 (1998): 377–406; E. W. Kelly, B. Greyson, and I. Stevenson, "Can Experiences Near Death Furnish Evidence of Life After Death?" *Omega* 40, no. 4 (1999–2000): 513–19.

Chapter 5: Proof #3: Blind Sight

1. K. Ring and S. Cooper, "Near-Death and Out-of-Body Experiences in the Blind: A Study of Apparent Eyeless Vision," *Journal of Near-Death*

Studies 16 (1998): 101–47. Results of this study were later presented in further detail: K. Ring and S. Cooper, *Mindsight: Near-Death and Out-of-Body Experiences in the Blind* (Palo Alto, CA: William James Center for Consciousness Studies, Institute of Transpersonal Psychology, 1999).

2. Ring and Cooper, *Mindsight,* 25.

3. Ring and Cooper, *Mindsight,* 46–47.

4. Ring and Cooper, *Mindsight,* 41–42.

5. Ring and Cooper, *Mindsight,* 151.

6. Ring and Cooper, *Mindsight,* 153.

7. Ring and Cooper, *Mindsight,* 157, 158, 163.

Chapter 6: Proof #4: Impossibly Conscious

1. B. Greyson, E. W. Kelly, and E. F. Kelly, "Explanatory Models for Near-Death Experiences," in *The Handbook of Near-Death Experiences: Thirty Years of Investigation,* ed. J. Holden, B. Greyson, and D. James (Westport, CT: Praeger Publishers, 2009), 226.

2. J. C. Eccles, *Evolution of the Brain, Creation of the Self* (London and New York: Routledge, 1991), 241.

3. Awakening (full or partial) under general anesthesia probably occurs in 1 to 3 in 1,000 cases: T. Heier and P. Steen, "Awareness in Anaesthesia: Incidence, Consequences and Prevention," *Acta Anaesthesiologica Scandinavica* 40 (1996): 1073–86; R. H. Sandin, G. Enlund, P. Samuelsson, and C. Lennmarken, "Awareness During Anaesthesia: A Prospective Case Study," *Lancet* 355 (2000): 707–11.

4. The experience of anesthesia awakening is very unlike what is described in NDEs: J. E. Osterman, J. Hopper, W. J. Heran, T. M. Keane, and B. A. van der Kolk, "Awareness Under Anesthesia and the Development of Posttraumatic Stress Disorder," *General Hospital Psychiatry* 23 (2001): 198–204; P. H. Spitelli, M. A. Holmes, and K. B. Domino, "Awareness During Anesthesia," *Anesthesiology Clinics of North America* 20 (2002): 555–70.

5. K. R. Nelson, M. Mattingley, S. A. Lee, and F. A. Schmitt, "Does the Arousal System Contribute to Near Death Experience?" *Neurology* 66 (2006): 1003–9.

6. J. Long and J. M. Holden, "Does the Arousal System Contribute to Near-Death and Out-of-Body Experiences? A Summary and Response," *Journal of Near-Death Studies* 25, no. 3 (2007): 135–69. This article is available through a link at http://www.nderf.org/evidence.

7. Eccles, *Evolution of the Brain, Creation of the Self,* 242.

Chapter 7: Proof #5: Perfect Playback

1. Personal communication from Raymond Moody, MD, to Paul Perry.

2. J. A. Long, "Life Review, Changed Beliefs, Universal Order and Purpose, and the Near-Death Experience: Part 4, Soulmates," Near-Death Experience Research Foundation (NDERF), http://www.nderf.org/purpose_lifereview.htm.

3. S. Blackmore, *Dying to Live: Near-Death Experiences* (New York: Prometheus, 1993).

4. S. Blackmore, "Near-Death Experiences: In or Out of the Body?" *Skeptical Inquirer* 16 (1991): 34–45, available at Susan Blackmore's website, http://www.susanblackmore.co.uk/Articles/si91nde.html.

5. E. W. Kelly, B. Greyson, and E. F. Kelly, "Unusual Experiences Near Death and Related Phenomena," in E. F. Kelly, E. W. Kelly, A. Crabtree, A. Gauld, M. Grosso, and B. Greyson, *Irreducible Mind: Toward a Psychology for the 21st Century* (Lanham, MD: Rowman & Littlefield, 2007), 382.

6. Kelly, Greyson, and Kelly, "Unusual Experiences," 382.

7. O. Blanke, S. Ortigue, T. Landis, and M. Seeck, "Stimulating Illusory Own Body Perceptions," *Nature* 419 (2002): 269–70.

8. O. Blanke, T. Landis, L. Spinelli, and M. Seeck, "Out-of-Body Experience and Autoscopy of Neurological Origin," *Brain* 127 (2004): 243–58.

9. J. Holden, J. Long, and J. MacLurg, "Out-of-Body Experiences: All in the Brain?" *Journal of Near-Death Studies* 25, no. 2 (2006): 99–107.

10. E. Rodin, "Comments on 'A Neurobiological Model for Near-Death Experiences,'" *Journal of Near-Death Studies* 7 (1989): 256.

11. Studies document that experiences associated with electrical brain stimulation and seizures are unlike NDEs: P. Gloor, A. Olivier, L. F. Quesney, F. Andermann, and S. Horowitz, "The Role of the Limbic System in Experiential Phenomena of Temporal Lobe Epilepsy," *An-*

nals of Neurology 12 (1982): 129–44; O. Devinsky, E. Feldmann, K. Burrowes, and E. Bromfield, "Autoscopic Phenomena with Seizures," *Archives of Neurology* 46 (1989): 1080–88.

Chapter 8: Proof #6: Family Reunion

1. E. W. Kelly, "Near-Death Experiences with Reports of Meeting Deceased People," *Death Studies* 25 (2001): 229–49.
2. In a large number of NDEs in the NDERF study, the NDEr encounters a being during the NDE that may seem familiar but that she or he does not recognize. The NDEr may later recognize the being they encountered as a deceased family member, often when looking at old family pictures after the NDE. This has been described by other NDE researchers: P. van Lommel, "About the Continuity of Our Consciousness," in *Brain Death and Disorders of Consciousness,* ed. C. Machado and D. A. Shewmon (New York: Springer, 2004), 115–32; E. F. Kelly, E. W. Kelly, A. Crabtree, A. Gauld, M. Grosso, and B. Greyson, *Irreducible Mind: Toward a Psychology for the 21st Century* (Lanham, MD: Rowman & Littlefield, 2007), 391.
3. In hallucinations, living people are more likely to be seen than deceased individuals: K. Osis and E. Haraldsson, *At the Hour of Death* (New York: Avon, 1977).

Chapter 9: Proof #7: From the Mouths of Babes

1. Stanford Encyclopedia of Philosophy, "Afterlife," http://plato.stanford .edu/entries/afterlife/.
2. Robert T. Carroll, "Near-Death Experience (NDE)," *The Skeptic's Dictionary:* http://www.skepdic.com/nde.html.
3. C. Sutherland, '"Trailing Clouds of Glory': The Near-Death Experiences of Western Children and Teens," in *The Handbook of Near-Death Experiences: Thirty Years of Investigation,* ed. J. Holden, B. Greyson, and D. James (Westport, CT: Praeger Publishers, 2009), 92, 93.
4. Other studies found that childhood NDEs are far more similar to adult NDEs than dissimilar: International Association for Near-Death Studies (IANDS), "Children's Near-Death Experiences," http://www.iands .org/nde_index/ndes/child.html; J. Holden, J. Long, and J. MacLurg,

"Characteristics of Western Near-Death Experiencers," in *The Handbook of Near-Death Experiences: Thirty Years of Investigation*, ed. J. Holden, B. Greyson, and D. James (Westport, CT: Praeger Publishers, 2009).

5. Holden, Long, and MacLurg, "Characteristics of Western Near-Death Experiencers," 114.

6. W. J. Serdahely, "A Comparison of Retrospective Accounts of Childhood Near-Death Experiences with Contemporary Pediatric Near-Death Experience Accounts," *Journal of Near-Death Studies* 9 (1991): 219.

7. B. Greyson, "Consistency of Near-Death Experience Accounts over Two Decades: Are Reports Embellished over Time?" *Resuscitation* 73 (2007): 407–11.

8. P. van Lommel, R. van Wees, V. Meyers, and I. Elfferich, "Near-Death Experience in Survivors of Cardiac Arrest: A Prospective Study in the Netherlands," *Lancet* 358 (2001): 2039–45.

9. M. L. Morse and P. Perry, *Transformed by the Light: The Powerful Effect of Near-Death Experiences on People's Lives* (New York: Villard Books, 1992).

Chapter 10: Proof #8: Worldwide Consistency

1. The distinction between Western and non-Western countries pertinent to the study of NDEs is presented here: J. Holden, J. Long, and J. MacLurg, "Characteristics of Western Near-Death Experiencers," in *The Handbook of Near-Death Experiences: Thirty Years of Investigation*, ed. J. Holden, B. Greyson, and D. James (Westport, CT: Praeger Publishers, 2009), 110.

2. For an overview of prior non-Western NDE research and some of the methodological problems of studying non-Western NDEs, see A. Kellehear, "Census of Non-Western Near-Death Experiences to 2005: Observations and Critical Reflections," in *Handbook of Near-Death Experiences*, ed. Holden, Greyson, and James.

3. Additional results and a more detailed discussion of the methodology from the NDERF cross-cultural study may be found at the link at http://www.nderf.org/evidence.

4. Kellehear, "Census of Non-Western Near-Death Experiences," 150.
5. B. Greyson, E. W. Kelly, and E. F. Kelly, "Explanatory Models for Near-Death Experiences," in *Handbook of Near-Death Experiences,* ed. Holden, Greyson, and James, 215.
6. Holden, Long, and MacLurg, "Characteristics of Western Near-Death Experiencers," 132.
7. It is worth emphasizing how important further research will be in studying non-Western NDEs and for the cross-cultural study of NDEs in general. There is a need for further high-quality research that includes publication of representative cross-cultural NDE narratives. In addition, there needs to be standard questions about NDE content, such as the NDE Scale, with the questions carefully translated into a variety of non-English languages, as NDERF has done. There also needs to be an effort to determine if there was a life-threatening event at the time of the experience. I hope that future cross-cultural NDE studies will be able to access NDErs in a variety of ways to help assure that the NDErs studied are reasonably representative of all NDErs in a particular culture. And, of course, we need to study many more non-Western NDErs, prospectively if possible, to include specific non-Western countries and subcultures. Finding non-Western NDErs in societies that have little contact with other cultures will be especially challenging but also especially important.
8. The archive of non-Western NDEs at NDERF that were shared in English or translated into English is found at http://www.nderf.org/non_western_ndes.htm.

Chapter 11: Proof #9: Changed Lives
1. P. M. H. Atwater, *The Big Book of Near-Death Experiences: The Ultimate Guide to What Happens When We Die* (Charlottesville, VA: Hampton Roads Publishing, 2007), 372.
2. One of the earliest studies of NDE aftereffects was by K. Ring, *Heading Toward Omega: In Search of the Meaning of the Near-Death Experience* (New York: William Morrow, 1984).
3. Two prospective studies of NDE in cardiac arrest survivors that assessed aftereffects were P. van Lommel, R. van Wees, V. Meyers, and

I. Elfferich, "Near-Death Experience in Survivors of Cardiac Arrest: A Prospective Study in the Netherlands," *Lancet* 358 (2001): 2039–45; J. Schwaninger, P. Eisenberg, K. Schechtman, and A. Weiss, "A Prospective Analysis of Near Death Experiences in Cardiac Arrest Patients," *Journal of Near-Death Studies* 20 (2002): 215–32.

4. Three studies found an increase in aftereffects among NDErs whose experiences included more detailed content, or "depth." In addition to van Lommel et al., "Survivors of Cardiac Arrest," and Schwaninger et al., "Cardiac Arrest Patients," see G. Groth-Marnat and R. Summers, "Altered Beliefs, Attitudes, and Behaviors Following Near-Death Experiences," *Journal of Humanistic Psychology* 38, no. 3 (1998): 110–25.

5. P. van Lommel, "About the Continuity of Our Consciousness," in *Brain Death and Disorders of Consciousness,* ed. C. Machado and D. A. Shewmon (New York: Springer, 2004), 118.

6. B. Greyson, "Near-Death Experiences and Anti-suicidal Attitudes," *Omega* 26 (1992–93): 81–89.

7. D. H. Rosen, "Suicide Survivors: A Follow-Up Study of Persons Who Survived Jumping from the Golden Gate and San Francisco–Oakland Bay Bridges," *Western Journal of Medicine* 122 (1975): 291.

8. P. Sartori, P. Badham, and P. Fenwick, "A Prospectively Studied Near-Death Experience with Corroborated Out-of-Body Perceptions and Unexplained Healing," *Journal of Near-Death Studies* 25 (2006): 69–84.

9. Scholarly literature discussing psychic NDE aftereffects includes R. L. Kohr, "Near-Death Experience and Its Relationship to Psi and Various Altered States," *Theta* 10 (1982): 50–53; R. L. Kohr, "Near-Death Experiences, Altered States, and Psi Sensitivity," *Anabiosis: The Journal for Near-Death Studies* 3 (1983): 157–76; B. Greyson, "Increase in Psychic Phenomena Following Near-Death Experiences," *Theta* 11 (1983): 26–29; C. Sutherland, "Psychic Phenomena Following Near-Death Experiences: An Australian Study," *Journal of Near-Death Studies* 8 (1989): 93–102.

10. Personal communication from anonymous near-death experiencer to Paul Perry.